CALL TO ACTION

CALL TO ACTION

Become the Man God Designed You to Be

Alun Ebenezer

Foreword by Gavin Peacock

Reformation Heritage Books
Grand Rapids, Michigan

Call to Action
© 2024 by Alun Ebenezer

All rights reserved. No part of this book may be used or reproduced in any manner whatsoever without written permission except in the case of brief quotations embodied in critical articles and reviews. Direct your requests to the publisher at the following addresses:

Reformation Heritage Books
3070 29th St. SE
Grand Rapids, MI 49512
616-977-0889
orders@heritagebooks.org
www.heritagebooks.org

Scripture taken from the New King James Version®. Copyright © 1982 by Thomas Nelson. Used by permission. All rights reserved.

Printed in the United States of America
24 25 26 27 28 29/10 9 8 7 6 5 4 3 2 1

Library of Congress Cataloging-in-Publication Data

Names: Ebenezer, Alun, author. | Peacock, Gavin, writer of foreword.
Title: Call to action : become the man God designed you to be / Alun
   Ebenezer ; foreword by Gavin Peacock.
Description: Grand Rapids, Michigan : Reformation Heritage Books,
   [2024] | Includes bibliographical references.
Identifiers: LCCN 2023056962 (print) | LCCN 2023056963 (ebook) |
   ISBN 9798886861013 (paperback) | ISBN 9798886861020 (epub)
Subjects: LCSH: Young men—Religious life—Juvenile literature. | Teenage
   boys—Religious life—Juvenile literature. | Christian teenagers—
   Religious life—Juvenile literature.
Classification: LCC BV4541.3 .E24 2024 (print) | LCC BV4541.3 (ebook) |
   DDC 248.8/32—dc23/eng/20240108
LC record available at https://lccn.loc.gov/2023056962
LC ebook record available at https://lccn.loc.gov/2023056963

For additional Reformed literature, request a free book list from Reformation Heritage Books at the above regular or email address

CONTENTS

Foreword.. vii
Introduction.. xi

1. Be... 1
2. Behold... 5
3. Call 9
4. Guard 13
5. Believe.. 17
6. Survey... 21
7. Discover 29
8. Trust 35
9. Repent... 38
10. Commune 40
11. Read 44
12. Think... 46
13. Pray.. 48
14. Deny 54
15. Kill... 57
16. Live 61
17. Work 64

- 18. Rest 68
- 19. Shine 71
- 20. View 73
- 21. Stand 77
- 22. Talk 81
- 23. Listen 84
- 24. Cast 87
- 25. Belong 89
- 26. Forget 92
- 27. Persevere 95
- 28. Lead 97
- 29. Go 101
- 30. Ask 105

Appendix: *A four-year reading plan for young Christian men* 107
Bibliography 111

FOREWORD

On his deathbed, King David spoke these words to his son Solomon: "I go the way of all the earth; be strong, therefore, and prove yourself a man. And keep the charge of the LORD your God: to walk in His ways, to keep His statutes, His commandments, His judgments, and His testimonies" (1 Kings 2:2–3). Last words are important, and David sees fit to tell his son, "Act like a man." But not just any man—a godly man. In our day, manhood is under attack. Many view it with suspicion and believe that masculinity is dangerous, oppressive, and "toxic." This has led to a generation of "men without chests," as C. S. Lewis put it. But God loves manhood and masculinity. He created mankind male and female (Gen. 1:27), and He teaches us in the Bible what it means to be a man.

But manhood is not just under attack—it is also not taught. This is because we live in a fatherless generation where dad has either been removed from his place in the center of the home, loving and leading his family, or has abdicated his role entirely. All children suffer in this sorry state of affairs, but boys suffer the most. I coached high school soccer for six years, and I would estimate that eighty percent of the young men in my charge during that time did not have a father or a father figure in their lives. In some cases, dad had left the home due to family strife; in others, he simply wasn't present in his son's life. My fellow coaches and I were their first example of what loving, masculine authority looked like and of how a man should behave.

The boys of today are the men of tomorrow. They need to be given a vision of their masculine potential. They need instruction and discipline to learn how to get there. And they need love to fuel them along the way. They need fathers to teach them how to be men of God, men who will be tomorrow's husbands and fathers. If you get the men, you get the home, the church, and the culture.

This is why the book in your hands is so important. It was written by a man with a father's heart for young men. Alun Ebenezer is a culture changer. In 2013, he became the founding headmaster of The Fulham Boys School, and, for nine years, he pioneered a unique brand of schooling with foundations in the Christian faith to educate and raise boys to be men. There are few who have given more thought and time to this task. To that end, he brings a wealth of knowledge on how young men think and what young men need. In thirty short chapters, he lays out a biblical vision of what a man of God looks like and what steps one must take to become that man.

Augustine, a church father and theologian, was a man who wasted his youth in the folly of sinful pursuits. He found no joy and no purpose in that way of life. One day, he was sitting in despair in his garden when he heard the voice of a young child in a house nearby saying, "Take up and read. Take up and read." He immediately went inside, turned to the book of Romans, and read these words:

> Let us walk properly, as in the day, not in revelry and drunkenness, not in lewdness and lust, not in strife and envy. But put on the Lord Jesus Christ, and make no provision for the flesh, to fulfill its lusts. (Rom. 13:13–14)

Augustine writes about this moment: "I had no wish to read more, nor need to do so. For, in an instant, as I came to the end of this sentence, it was as though the light of confidence flooded into my heart, and all the darkness of doubt was dispelled." Augustine turned to God and His Word at age thirty-two, and he became a man.

Young man, don't waste your youth as Augustine did. Life is short. Don't put off until tomorrow what you can do today. Take up and read this book you hold—let Alun Ebenezer teach you through the Scriptures what it means to be a man even as he points you to the true Man, Jesus Christ. The apostle John writes, "Jesus came out, wearing the crown of thorns and the purple robe. And Pilate said to them, 'Behold the Man!'" (John 19:5). Pilate was mocking. But Jesus actually is *the* Man. A king who died for His people. A shepherd who was slain for His sheep. A husband who died for His Bride. He has taken initiative, and His actions have provided salvation and hope, that you would be the man you were made to be through faith in Him.

— Gavin Peacock

INTRODUCTION

This book is for young men. Young men who are determined to become real men. Christian men. This does not happen automatically. You must be proactive and take action. There are thirty chapters, one for each day of the month. In every chapter, there is an action to help you become the man of God you are required to be, the man that our churches, schools, universities, workplaces, families, communities, and countries need you to be.

It is important to say at the outset that I have failed at almost every action I discuss (sometimes badly!), which is the reason I wrote this book. I urge you to learn from my mistakes and to take the actions I wish I had. As I look back, I can testify that God knows best and that His ways are perfect (Ps. 18:30). His design and His plan really are to prosper you and not to harm you (Jer. 29:11).

I understand that, overall, young men are not big readers (although you do need to be—see chapter 10!). With that in mind, some chapters are quite short, others a bit longer, but each chapter will take you ten minutes or fewer to read. You will need your Bible alongside this book, and I encourage you to take the time to look up the passages referenced in each chapter.

So, gentlemen, if you are ready, buckle up. Let's begin.

1

BE

The first action is to *be*. Be a man (1 Cor. 16:13).

This opening chapter is quite technical. It's a real hot potato, one that flies in the face of modern thinking and that may even sound controversial. In fact, if you adopt the Christian view of manhood, you may very well be accused of bigotry, sexism, chauvinism, or worse. So, as you read this first chapter, hang in there, be brave, engage your brain, and really think!

The Bible is clear that boys and girls are different. Not better or worse, not superior or inferior, just different. According to Genesis 1:27, "God created man in His own image; in the image of God He created him; male and female He created them." Boys and girls are created differently. This has been confirmed by those who have researched the male and female brains, much less anyone who has ever spent any time with boys and girls. Moreover, whenever anyone hears of a newborn baby, the first question he asks is, "Is it a boy or a girl?"

However, the distinction between the sexes is being blurred today. We are taught that gender is fluid and that you are what you feel. According to transgenderism (the belief that someone is not the same gender that he or she was at birth), God may have mistakenly put an opposite-sex "spirit" into the wrong body, an internal sense of gender that may or may not align with one's biological sex. The "real you" is who you feel yourself to be on the inside. This means that subjective feelings override objective, biological, genetic reality. A boy or a girl may simply be trapped in the wrong body.

In recent years, this has been accepted as fact by much of the public and has been embraced and promoted by the mainstream media and celebrities. Activists are pushing society toward accepting transgenderism unquestioningly and shutting down the essential debate surrounding it. Instead of providing transgender people with the support they need to embrace the bodies they were born with, society is compounding their confusion, leading to harmful consequences. Drastic and dangerous treatments are being promoted, such as puberty-blocking drugs, hormone therapy, and "gender-affirming" surgeries. Many go on to regret these treatments. The impact on young people is particularly concerning, as the long-term effects are still unknown.

The reality is that, however we feel, a man cannot become a woman, and a woman cannot become a man. It is not loving to "affirm" the idea that a person is "trapped in the wrong body." It is dangerous, both physically and psychologically. Male chromosomes cannot be changed into female chromosomes. Altering one's appearance, cosmetically or surgically, cannot change one's underlying biological makeup. In short, psychology cannot override biology.

As Christians, however, we must accept and embrace the reality that there are precious persons who genuinely struggle with gender dysphoria—a condition where a person senses that his or her gender identity (how the person feels about being male or female) may not align with his or her biological sex, resulting in emotional distress. These people are hurting and need to know that, while we may not agree with them, as Christians, we love them, we're there for them, we're ready to listen to them and seek to understand the pain they are facing, and we deeply desire what is best for them.

The Christian worldview can fully explain why people experience gender dysphoria. As a result of the fall, creation has been disrupted—it is not the way it once was, nor the way it will eventually be in the new creation (Genesis 3; Romans 8; Revelation 21). No part of our existence in the universe has been left undisturbed by sin's effects. This means that the brokenness of creation reaches into every corner of our lives—even our minds and hearts. We are all made in God's image, but we all struggle with the brokenness of our bodies, desires, and thoughts in different ways and to different degrees. So, in this created, but broken, world, we understand that not all identities or feelings are to be accepted, because we are all guided by a mixture of righteous and broken desires.

As Christian men (even though it might be particularly hard for some of us), we must acknowledge that God made us—He gets the ultimate say in who we are. For those who do not struggle in this area, we need to speak with compassion, remembering that Jesus did not seek to win debates.

He sought to love people. And as his followers, so must we. Importantly, we must also realize that being a man does not mean being a certain type of man. Some men are sporty, others not. Some are more sensitive, others less. The call is to *be* a man, not a stereotypical macho man.

2

BEHOLD

One of the hardest things to be today is a young man. Right now, it is open season on manhood, and to some extent, this is understandable. At our worst, we men are power hungry, aggressive, and entitled. We demean and abuse women, we're bad role models for our children, we're addicted to screens and pornography, and we can't be trusted. We engage in behaviors that have made the streets unsafe after dark, we have developed rape culture at some of our "top" schools, and we are guilty of widespread sexual misconduct—so much so that when women tell their stories of harassment, many others have said #MeToo. Many believe that masculinity is "toxic" and that the time has come to fundamentally change how "boys will be boys."

So, what should a man be like? A woman? Is that the answer? Feminize boys? Over the years, many frustrated schoolteachers have said to boys, "Why can't you be more like the girls?!" Everyone's invited to have their say on this, and different groups use social media to push their agendas forward. But at such a watershed moment in the reconstruction of twenty-first-century man, we should do what Pontius

Pilate told the first-century crowd in Jerusalem to do: *behold* the Man (John 19:5), the Man who sixteenth-century reformer Martin Luther called the "proper man."

The Man was Jesus of Nazareth. He was no superman, but He was a real man. He looked like a man, indistinguishable from other Israeli men. He developed like a normal child—He learned to speak, read, and write, and He went to school. He experienced tiredness, loneliness, thirst, hunger, sorrow, laughter, and love. He suffered, bled, and died.

He was lower working class. The oldest of at least eight children, He was raised in a small, backwater village in north Palestine, a place infamous for its wildness and wickedness. In tight, cramped conditions, where families have misunderstandings and where tempers fray, He lived in a home made of mud and branches, comprising one large room, with a goat, a cow, or a donkey at one end, and a raised platform where the family slept on mats at the other.

Growing up, He played on the streets of Nazareth with the other children; spoke with a heavy northern accent; learned a trade from his supposed father, who was a carpenter; and spent most of His working life doing building and repair work around Nazareth. He got angry and spoke out against wrongdoing, but He was never harsh or cruel. He was unselfish—He never responded to provocation, nor did He engage in self-justification. He always did the right thing, not the easiest thing. He couldn't be bought or schmoozed, and He chose a company of fishermen and outcasts rather than the great and successful men of this world. He was kind and full of compassion. As He hung on a Roman cross, dying in agony, He thought about His mother and arranged for her to be supported. Despite being busy and tired, He felt sorry for people, listened to their problems, gave them time and attention, and dealt with them tenderly.

Children wanted to be with Him, and in stark contrast to the thinking of His day, He had a high regard for women. He relied on their help and assigned them a place of honor. In a culture where women were not trusted to give testimony in a court of law, it was women who were by His cross at the end of His life and the first witnesses of His resurrection. Nothing and no one has done more for the dignity of women than this man.

To show His disciples what greatness looked like, He put on a slave's apron, poured water into a basin, and washed their feet—feet that had walked in sandals along dirty, dusty Palestinian roads. He knew and faced all the temptations of working men, but He didn't sin. According to those closest to Him, he never did anything wrong. His enemies could find no fault in Him (John 19:4). Even the one who handed Him over to His enemies, who knew Him as well as anyone, later confessed, "I have sinned by betraying innocent blood" (Matt. 27:4).

He respected His parents and dutifully served His family. He may have delayed His entry into public life because His father died when He was young—as the oldest in the family, He would have assumed His father's responsibilities until the next brother was mature enough to take over. He is a peerless teacher of the ages and taught with authority. Those who heard Him said, "No man ever spoke like this Man!" (John 7:46). He never paraded His wisdom, but He combined simplicity and profundity so that "the common people heard Him gladly" (Mark 12:37).

But this Man didn't come into the world just to be an example. He came to actually sort out the mess men have made. He came not to judge but to save. And He did it by being stripped, tied up, beaten, punched, spat on, whipped, laughed at, and finally, nailed to a Roman cross in a dump outside the city wall of Jerusalem. Here, He took the punishment for, and dealt with, all the mess, guilt, shame, hurt, filth, anger, and sin of the world.

He has forgiven the young men we once were. He's an example of the men we should be, and He helps us to become those men.

3

CALL

The Bible's central message is that "we must be saved" (Acts 4:12). "Salvation" is a picture-word that signifies deliverance from jeopardy and misery to safety. The Bible is clear that all men are sinners (Rom. 3:23) and that the wages of sin is death (Rom. 6:23). Our only hope of escaping eternal damnation is salvation.

Sin

As much as it offends us, we know we are sinners. We like to think of ourselves at our best, but the real us appears when we repeatedly do what comes "naturally." Think about what you are like when you are by yourself, what you enjoy doing when you are left to your own devices, how angry you get, how dirty your mind is, and how many shameful things you have done (or would have done given the chance!). Think about your Internet history. Think about your language, your pride, and your laziness. That's the real you: a sinner. *So,* you may be thinking, *what's the problem?*

Death

The problem is that we have to die. The cold reality of our

world is that, as Usain Bolt put it, "nobody ever makes it out alive." Like Dylan Thomas, we can "rage, rage against the dying of the light,"[1] but ultimately, we all end up dead. The reason we must be saved is because death is not the end.

Judgment

After death comes the judgment (Heb. 9:27). Whether you like it or not, and whether you believe it or not, we will all stand before the judgment seat of God. Not the judgment seat of public opinion. Not the judgment seat of modern thinking. Not the judgment seat of social media. The judgment seat of God. People who stand before this judgment seat in their sin will be condemned to an eternal hell. This is why we must be saved.

Impossible

But it is impossible for us to save ourselves (Matt. 19:25–26). God's standard is absolute perfection. To be right with Him, we have to keep the Ten Commandments—not only outwardly but also inwardly (Matt. 5:21–30). That is, we must never lie, never lust, never lose our temper, never be unkind or selfish. We must love God with all our heart, soul, mind, and strength and love our neighbor as much as we love ourselves (Matt. 22:37–39). It is impossible! Every one of us has broken these commandments and continues to break them every day. And there is nothing we can do to take away our guilt, right our wrongs, or stop our sin.

---

1. Dylan Thomas, "Do Not Go Gentle into That Good Night," https://www.poetryfoundation.org/poems/46569/do-not-go-gentle-into-that-good-night.

Only one person can save us, and that's the Man we *beheld* in the last chapter. He has promised to save anyone and everyone who *calls* out to him. According to Acts 2:21, "Whoever calls on the name of the LORD shall be saved."

Manasseh

Maybe you think you're too sinful for God to hear your call. Well, consider Manasseh. He was king of Judah for fifty-five years and was an awful, wicked man. He was brought up in a godly, Christian home, but he turned his back on God completely and led the whole nation into sin for decades. He reintroduced Baal worship, which was a sex cult (2 Kings 21:3); installed a pornographic image in the temple (2 Kings 21:7); built altars to the sun, moon, and stars in both courts of the temple (2 Kings 21:5); and engaged with fortune-telling, omens, sorcery, mediums, and necromancers (2 Kings 21:6). He killed so many people, including God's prophets, that he filled Jerusalem from end to end with blood (2 Kings 21:16). According to tradition, he sawed the prophet Isaiah in two (Heb. 11:37). Chillingly, he even killed his own son (2 Kings 21:6). He ignored God (2 Kings 21:9), trampled on His Word (2 Kings 21:7–8), and provoked Him on purpose (2 Kings 21:6).

Nevertheless, "The LORD spoke to Manasseh" (2 Chron. 33:10). Incredibly, God reached out and spoke to this awful monster. Even though Manasseh ignored Him at first (2 Chron. 33:10), God persisted and did whatever it took to get his attention. The passage continues, "Therefore the LORD brought upon them the captains of the army of the king of Assyria, who took Manasseh with hooks, bound him with bronze fetters, and carried him off to Babylon" (2 Chron. 33:11).

The Assyrians were the terrors of the ancient world, and God used them to take Manasseh captive. They carried him off with hooks through his nose and lips, treating him like a beast. For twelve years he was tortured in a Babylonian dungeon. He was placed in a huge, bronze pot in the desert—during the day it heated up to an unbearable temperature, and at night it froze.

In this agony and distress, as he thought about all he had done, Manasseh called out to God (2 Chron. 33:12). Maybe the Scriptures he had been taught as a child came back to him. He could never right all his wrongs, and he had nothing to offer God. But he "prayed to Him" (2 Chron. 33:13). He called out to God for forgiveness, and God heard him: "He received his entreaty, heard his supplication, and brought him back to Jerusalem" (2 Chron. 33:13). Manasseh's cry moved God (see also 2 Chron. 33:19). Despite all that he had done, God had mercy on him and saved him.

Manasseh's God is our God. He still speaks to people and saves all who call out to Him. He is speaking to you now as you read these words. He has spoken to many of you hundreds and thousands of times before. He has put you in families where the Bible is loved and read, and in churches where the Bible is faithfully preached. He has given you friends who talk to you about Him. You have been to camps and conferences. Through all of this, God is speaking to you. So, whatever you have done, and however bad a state you are in, *call* out to God to save you, with full confidence that whoever calls out to Him will be saved.

4

GUARD

It is vital for young men to *guard* their hearts. Proverbs 4:23 says, "Keep [guard] your heart with all diligence, for out of it spring the issues of life."

Heart

The heart is the very center of a person. Everything we think, say, feel, and do comes from our hearts. The problem is that, by nature, our hearts are bad. They are deceitful above all things and desperately wicked (Jer. 17:9). Our hearts are dull (Matt. 13:15), proud (Luke 1:51), hard (Rom. 2:5), lustful (Rom. 1:24), and rebellious against God (Matt. 15:8).

Our fundamental problem is not bad parents, bad schools, bad friends, bad circumstances, or bad politicians. Our biggest problem is not "out there," but inside of us (Mark 7:20–23). The heart of our problem is the problem of our heart.

Regeneration

So, before we can guard our hearts, God needs to set our hearts right. We need a new heart. Theologians call this "regeneration." It is essential to becoming a Christian, and it is impossible without the work of the Holy Spirit. The Bible says that we are all "dead in trespasses and sins" (Eph. 2:1). Only the Holy Spirit can give us life. According to Packer, regeneration is "God renovating the heart, the core of a person's being, by implanting a new principle of desire, purpose and action."[1] First, the Holy Spirit convicts us of our sin and shows us our need for salvation. He then points us to Jesus Christ and gives us the faith to believe in Him. Once this happens, young Christian men need to do all they can to guard their hearts.

Dangers
There are particular dangers of which young men need to be aware. These include sex, pornography, spending too much time playing video games (particularly some unhelpful games), wasting time, becoming addicted to screens and social media, laziness, immaturity, giving in to peer pressure, wanting and abusing power, bullying, anger, and violence.

Discipline
Young men need to be disciplined in these areas, especially the ones with which they personally struggle. Know yourself, and don't put yourself in situations where you will give in to temptation. Make a covenant, or promise, with your eyes not to look at anything you shouldn't (Job 31:1; Prov. 4:25). Be careful what you watch on television and online. Don't give

---

1. J. I. Packer, *Concise Theology: A Guide to Historic Christian Beliefs* (London: Inter-Varsity Press, 1994), 157.

in to the "second look." Put your phone in a different room when you go to bed. Use your computer in places where others can see you. Watch the way you speak (Ps. 34:13; Prov. 4:24). Don't swear, but tell the truth, and avoid gossip, slander, and dirty talk. Think about the places you go and how you spend your time (Prov. 4:26; Eccl. 5:1). Limit the amount of time you spend playing video games.

Hide

Do not harden your heart by resisting the Word of God. Instead, imitate the psalmist and hide God's Word in your heart so that you will not sin against Him (Ps. 119:11). This involves reading your Bible every day and sitting under good preaching every week—do what the Scriptures say, however difficult it may be.

Think

To help guard your heart, think about the love of God. When Joseph was tempted by Potiphar's wife, he had such a strong sense of God's love in his heart that even this alluring temptation could not sway him. He said, "How then can I do this great wickedness, and sin against God?" (Gen. 39:9).

Think about death, judgment, and hell. Think about the beauty of holiness—Christ died for us so that we might be "holy and without blame before Him" (Eph. 1:4). Think about where temptation leads and how it makes you feel after you have given in. Sin feels so good at the time, but it ruins lives, divides families, and causes untold pain. The journalist Malcolm Muggeridge once met a woman who, he was told, had slept with the writer H. G. Wells. He asked her how it had happened. She told him that Wells approached her at a party and said, "Shall we go upstairs and do something funny?" "And was it funny?" asked Muggeridge. "No sir, it was not funny," she replied. "That evening has caused me more misery than any other evening in my life."[2]

Think about your privileges as a Christian: reconciliation with God, adoption into His family, the hope of heaven, and the peace of God that Paul tells us will guard our hearts and minds (Phil. 4:7).

---

2. Vaughan Roberts, *Battles Christians Face: Tackling Big Issues with Confidence*, 2nd ed. (Milton Keynes, UK: Authentic Media, 2013), 32.

5

BELIEVE

....

We live in a time when people do not know what or who to believe. Life seems full of broken promises and fake news, but the Bible is trustworthy. The Christian faith is the truth (Gal. 2:5; Eph. 1:13). The Lord Jesus came to show us the truth (John 1:17)—not only does He tell the truth, but He is the Truth personified (John 14:6). You can confidently *believe* on the Lord Jesus Christ and trust what the Bible says. But how can we be sure?

Eyewitnesses

First, there were eyewitnesses to all the things Jesus of Nazareth said and did—especially His death and resurrection—some of whom recorded their accounts in the Bible. Over the years in my job, I have sometimes had to sort out fights between students. If a fight has occurred at lunchtime, I have to interview students to find out what happened. Everyone wants to leave class to tell me about it. However, most of them have only heard what others have said, so they are promptly sent back to class. But then someone comes to my office and says, "Sir, I saw everything. I saw the punches flying;

I heard the hair being torn; I smelled the sweat and saw the blood. I saw everything, Sir. I couldn't have been closer to the action—I was ringside!"

The men who recorded Jesus's life, death, and resurrection could not have been closer to the action. They were "ringside." They concluded that Jesus was the Truth, the Son of God, and the Savior of the world. They were so convinced that they were prepared to die for Him. Even the centurion who oversaw His crucifixion said, "Certainly this was a righteous Man!" (Luke 23:47).

Authority

Second, we can be sure Jesus is the Truth because the Bible says so. The Bible was written by more than forty people over a period of 1,500 years, and yet there is a remarkable unity and coherence throughout the whole book. This means it must be the work of a single, divine author. According to Paul, "All Scripture is given by inspiration of God, and is profitable for doctrine, for reproof, for correction, for instruction in righteousness" (2 Tim. 3:16). That is, God breathed out the Bible. All its prophecies to date have been fulfilled, and its message is still relevant thousands of years later. As Peter writes, "Prophecy never came by the will of man, but holy men of God spoke as they were moved by the Holy Spirit" (2 Peter 1:21).

The Test of Time

We can be confident that the Bible is true because it has stood the test of time. It is no novelty. It has been subjected to persecution and ridicule throughout the ages, but it still survives today. Men have tried to disprove the Bible, but it still holds true. In my job, I have also had to interview students who have done something wrong. Nearly all students will, at first, deny any wrongdoing. And so, my task is to cross-examine them, to come at them from different angles. Eventually the truth comes out. The Bible, meanwhile, has been cross-examined for thousands of years. Men have come at it from different angles, but it is still true! Even the Jewish historian Josephus wrote of Jesus Christ:

> About this time lived Jesus, a wise man, if indeed one ought to call him a man. For he was an achiever of extraordinary deeds…. Pilate condemned him to be crucified, those who had come to love him did not cease to do so; for he appeared to them on the third day restored to life.[1]

A Careful and Thorough Historian

After the apostle Paul, Luke wrote most of the New Testament (namely, the gospel of Luke and Acts). At the beginning of his gospel, he describes the painstaking research he carried out and all the eyewitnesses with whom he consulted in order to demonstrate the certainty of his account (Luke 1:1–4). These eyewitnesses would no doubt have included the apostles (Luke 1:2), including Peter, John, and James, the Lord's brother. James would have given him, among other things,

---

1. Paul L. Maier, trans., *Josephus: The Essential Writings* (Grand Rapids: Kregel, 1988), 264–65.

firsthand information about the ascension (Acts 1), the day of Pentecost (Acts 2), and Stephen's martyrdom (Acts 7).

Luke's sources also would have included the elderly Mary, the mother of the Lord Jesus, as well as her close friends and relatives. Luke could have talked to her while he was in Jerusalem (Acts 21:17). She would have told him all the things that she had treasured up in her heart (Luke 2:19). Most of the five hundred to whom Christ appeared after His resurrection were still alive (1 Cor. 15:6) and could have provided Luke with information. Not to mention Luke's own diary. The biographical details in the "we" sections in Acts (16:10–17; 20:5–15; 21:1–18; 27:1–37; 28:1–16) show that Luke had abundant opportunity to collect the information for his book. Paul and Silas would have given him a lot of details, and in Palestine he would have come in contact with the chief characters of the early church.

Powerful
The Bible has also powerfully influenced the lives of millions of people and has transformed whole communities, whole countries, and even the whole of civilization. In the sixteenth-century Reformation, it transformed Europe. The German Reformer Martin Luther, talking of the Reformation and his part in it, said, "I simply taught, preached, wrote God's Word: otherwise I did nothing. And then, while I slept or drank Wittenburg beer with my Philip of Amsdorf the Word so greatly weakened the papacy that never a prince or emperor did such damage to it. I did nothing: the Word did it all."

6

SURVEY

....

Christianity is about a Savior—one who can save to the uttermost all those who come to Him. To paraphrase Luther, "When I look at myself, I don't know how I could be saved. When I look at the Savior, I don't know how I could be lost." The Savior is the Lord Jesus Christ, the Son of God, who accomplished salvation by dying on a cross. This cross is the master theme of the Christian gospel. In his letter to the Galatians, the apostle Paul writes, "But God forbid that I should boast except in the cross of our Lord Jesus Christ, by whom the world has been crucified to me, and I to the world" (Gal. 6:14). Similarly, he tells the Corinthians, "For I determined not to know anything among you except Jesus Christ and Him crucified" (1 Cor. 2:2).

In what is arguably one of the greatest hymns ever written, Isaac Watts describes himself surveying the cross. To "survey" means to look closely and examine. So, today's action is to do just that: to "survey the wondrous cross."

The Cross

The Lord Jesus was crucified at a place called Calvary, also known as Golgotha, which was a dump outside the city gates of Jerusalem. By the time the Roman soldiers had walked Him through the city streets to get there, he had been stripped, tied up, beaten, punched, spat on, flogged, and ridiculed. Jesus started carrying His cross to Calvary (John 19:17), but, weakened by His beatings, He collapsed and fell under its weight and was unable to carry it any further. A man called Simon of Cyrene was ordered by the Roman soldiers to carry Jesus's cross. In his gospel, Mark indicates that Jesus was so weak that He Himself also needed to be supported (Mark 15:22). It is beyond comprehension that the One who was supported by the Roman soldiers was at the same time upholding the cosmos (Col. 1:17).

It isn't really surprising that Jesus collapsed. He was no doubt dehydrated. He had had no food or drink since the Last Supper with His disciples, and then He endured the agony in Gethsemane, where He actually sweat blood (Luke 22:44). He was then arrested by a mob with torches, lanterns, and swords. He stood trial before Annas, Caiaphas, Pilate, and Herod, before being sent back to Pilate. He was marched from one place to the other, chained, bound, and roughly handled. He even had a crown of thorns squeezed on His head.

When Jesus eventually got to Calvary, the soldiers laid Him on the cross and nailed Him to it. He was probably naked. Romans crucified people naked, whereas Jews, for the sake of dignity, wanted those who were crucified to be clothed. The fact that the soldiers gambled for Christ's clothes (Matt. 27:35), however, suggests He was naked.

The soldiers then would have lifted the cross and dropped it into a prepared socket. Every bone in Jesus's body would have jolted, and His nerves would have shivered with the excruciating pain. Crucifixion is one of the worst forms of punishment ever devised. Indeed, the word "excruciating" has the same root as "crucifixion." Cicero, a Roman writer, declared crucifixion to be the most cruel and shameful of all punishments. He wrote, "Let it never come near the body of a Roman citizen; nay, not even his thoughts or eyes or ears." The Romans invented crucifixion, but it was intended to be used only on non-Romans. It was reserved as a punishment for the grossest crimes and for slaves. In short, it was disgraceful (Gal. 3:13; 5:11; Heb. 12:2).

Jesus was in a terrible state on the cross. People were astonished at Him—He was so disfigured that He was beyond human likeness (Isa. 52:14). He looked like a thing of horror, like a lump of flesh, one that could be an animal or a human. People hid their faces from Him (Isa. 53:3). He was crushed, wounded, and pierced (Isa. 53:5).

But the gospel writers show marvelous restraint in their accounts of the crucifixion. All four of them simply say, "they crucified him" (Matt. 27:35; Mark 15:24; Luke 23:33; John 19:18). They don't dwell on the torment Jesus endured. They are good historians and avoid embellishing any of the details. They are not interested in what it was like for Him to suffer but why He suffered. The important thing is the significance of His death.

Propitiation

On the cross, the Lord Jesus suffered hell for all those who would trust in Him. But how, you may ask, could six hours of torture accomplish this? How could the millions of sins of millions of people, each one deserving eternal damnation, be paid for in a few hours on a cross, however painful they may have been? I don't know, but Peter tells us that, for God, a day is like a thousand years, and a thousand years are like a day (2 Peter 3:8). So, maybe it was something like Narnia. In C. S. Lewis's *The Lion, the Witch and the Wardrobe*, four English children pass through a magic wardrobe and enter a land called Narnia. They feel like they are there for thousands of years, but when they come back through the wardrobe into England, they have only been away for a few seconds. In Narnia, time is not the same. I think this is what happened at Calvary. On earth, the crucifixion took several hours, but as Christ went into the darkness, He left time, entered eternity, and suffered an eternal hell.

The fact that Jesus Christ went through hell shows just how much sin angers God. It is not the sort of anger that makes someone fly off the handle, but a just, steady, constant, burning anger. On the cross, Jesus was turning away this anger. He was extinguishing the wrath of God the Father. The Bible uses the word "propitiation" to describe this work (1 John 2:2). Christ bore the wrath of God so that God could become "propitious," or favorably disposed, toward us. It is not just that the Lord Jesus stops God from being angry with us, but that He enables us to enjoy God's favor. Indeed, forgiving our sins isn't just a legal dilemma for God. The problem is not merely that His justice needs to be satisfied—sin must be punished, and someone has to pay that punishment—but also that sin opposes the very character and being of God. He is offended by it, and He is angry with us. If we are to be at peace with God, then His anger needs to be quenched. Christ has quenched this anger, allowing God's favor to rest upon those who trust in Him.

At Calvary, Jesus bore the sins of many in His body on the tree (Isa. 53:12; Heb. 9:28; 1 Peter 2:24). In fact, He was made to be sin for us (2 Cor. 5:21). On the cross, He was cursed, vile, foul, and repulsive. We all know the awful feeling of guilt, but we cannot begin to imagine how Christ must have felt when he took the blame for the sins of millions.

Atonement

My sins have not just angered God—they have also put me in His debt. This is a debt that I would spend eternity in hell paying off, but by shedding His blood on the cross, Jesus made full atonement for it. Atonement means "a making at one." It's a process of bringing those who are estranged into unity. In theology, it denotes the work of Christ in dealing with our sin and in bringing sinners into a right relationship with God.

The atonement Jesus made was vicarious, that is, He made atonement in the place of others. On the cross, He was putting right, making up, paying a debt on behalf of all those who trust in Him. All our sins were laid on Christ (Isa. 53:6, 12; John 1:29; 2 Cor. 5:21; Gal. 3:13; Heb. 9:28; 1 Peter 2:24). He took upon Himself my sins and paid for them all—every last one of them. The secret ones, the "little" ones, the shameful ones, the ones I commit time and time and time again. The ones I have forgotten. The willful ones. He paid for them all.

Justification

Through the blood of Jesus, everything that was necessary to put us right with God has been done. The Bible calls this "justification." Justification frees a person from the guilt and condemnation of sin. It is a judicial act of God wherein He pardons sinners. He declares the sinner righteous and perfect in His sight.

For me to be right with God, I must keep God's law perfectly—in thought, word, and deed. But this is impossible. I break it every day, and there is nothing I can do to atone for all the sins I have committed. All I can offer God is a bad record. Far from putting me right with God, the law and my attempts to keep it confirm that I am guilty and that I deserve God's wrath. It is impossible for me to be justified before God by the law, but based on what Christ did at Calvary, God is able to justify me.

Justification doesn't actually change me. It is a declaration by God concerning me. It is not something I earn by what I do but rather something that is done for me. I have only been made righteous in the sense that God regards me as righteous and pronounces me righteous. As soon as I am justified, I am right with God.

On the cross, Jesus Christ was my substitute. In a legal sense, in God's eyes, He became me, and I became Him. Jesus lived a perfect life. This is called His "active obedience." By trusting Him, the life He lived becomes mine; His righteousness becomes mine. I take off my sinful life and put it on Jesus, and He clothes me with His righteousness. When you stand before God, whose lifelong record would you rather rely on, yours or Christ's?

If you are a Christian, you do not need to worry about standing before God at the judgment. You will stand before Him, clothed in His righteousness, as if you've done nothing wrong. We are accepted by God in Christ (Eph. 1:6).

One day I will stand before God. There will be many people present—family, friends, neighbors, classmates, coworkers—who could point to my sins and argue that I should not be allowed into heaven. Then there is my conscience, which can bring to mind the things I've thought and done that no one else knows. That will definitely condemn me! Further, God's law shows me that I've failed on every point. The Devil, through all of these things, will accuse me. But on that awesome day when I stand before the Judge of all the earth, Jesus Christ will plead for me. He will stand with me, and when the Devil, the law, my conscience, my past, and everyone who knows me condemn me, He will say, as it were, "Look at those three crosses. On the middle one, I took all your sins upon Myself and paid for every one of them!"

Forgiveness and Cleansing

While He hung on the cross, the Lord Jesus Christ prayed to God the Father: "Father, forgive them, for they do not know what they do" (Luke 23:34). The Greek can be translated, "Jesus kept on praying," "forgive them, forgive them, forgive them." Jesus was on the cross to bring forgiveness to people who didn't deserve it. Forgiveness is never easy. As C. S. Lewis wrote, "Every one says forgiveness is a lovely idea, until they have something to forgive."[1] The offended have been hurt badly, and that hurt has to be dealt with. On the cross, Jesus dealt with all my offenses against God so that all my sin can be forgiven. My gossip, adultery, hatred, lying, lust, spitefulness, anger, laziness—all my iniquity has been laid on Him (Isa. 53:5).

Christ's death on the cross also means that we can be made clean. As John writes, "the blood of Jesus Christ His Son cleanses us from all sin" (1 John 1:7). Our dirty hearts and filthy lives can be made clean.

Blanchard wrote that, one time, when he was leading a tour of the Holy Land, he left Jerusalem by the Damascus Gate and turned right by the bus station.[2] As he looked at the buses for the destination sign he needed, his eyes caught sight of a little hill just behind the station. It was "Gordon's Calvary." He thought that he might actually be looking at the place of the skull, Golgotha (Matt. 27:33), the very spot where, two thousand years ago, the Lord Jesus Christ bore the penalty for every sin that was to stain and scar his life. Mr. Blanchard said that he stood there looking at it with tears of gratitude running down his face.

Gentlemen, I encourage you to regularly *survey* that same wondrous cross.

---

1. C. S. Lewis, *Mere Christianity* (New York: HarperCollins, 2009), 115.
2. John Blanchard, *Major Points from the Minor Prophets* (Darlington, UK: Evangelical Press, 2012), 50.

7

DISCOVER

Today's action is to *discover*—to discover who God is and what He is really like. Lots of people assume they know what God is like, and their view of Him is based on things they have heard about Him, their own upbringing, or even their own personality, temperament, or experiences. But it is important to discover what God is actually like, and the way to do that is to read the Bible, where He has revealed Himself to us.

We must establish at the outset that there is *only one God*, and that this one God is *three persons*: God the Father, God the Son, and God the Holy Spirit. This is known as the Trinity—it is impossible to explain. But just because we cannot explain it, that does not mean it is untrue. In fact, the Trinity is one reason that convinces me Christianity *is* true, as no human being could make it up. In our attempt to understand God, we must not shrink Him down to the size of our minds. We must have a big view of God. To paraphrase Augustine, "If you think you have grasped God, it is not God you have grasped." In a short chapter like this, it is impossible to do justice to the full character of God, but we will draw attention to some of His attributes and explain a few of them in more detail.

God is *omnipotent*, which means He is all powerful (Isaiah 40). He is the *Creator* of heaven and earth (Gen. 1:1). It is very hard to comprehend God's power, but think of it like this: We live on a planet called Earth, which orbits a star called the sun at a distance of some ninety-three million miles. Our sun belongs to a galaxy called the Milky Way, which contains over one hundred billion other stars. Our galaxy is not alone in the universe but is just one of over one hundred billion other galaxies. And God made all this—out of nothing—by simply speaking![1]

Or imagine that you get into a car and want to travel to the sun. Let's say that it is a very fast car—you travel at 150 miles per hour—and that you never stop for fuel, food, or rest. At this rate, it would take you seventy years to reach the sun! You then head off for the next nearest star, Alpha Centauri, some four light years away. You travel at the same speed, and fifteen million years later, you are approaching the outskirts of this star! God made all this and beyond.[2]

God is *sovereign* over all things. Nothing is outside His control. He is the God of "macro" sovereignty, that is, the big things. Nations and kings rise and fall at His command (Job 12:23). He is also the God of "micro" sovereignty. Every minute detail is known to Him. He is in control of your life. He knew you before you were born (Jer. 1:5) and has numbered all your days (Ps. 90:3–6). Abraham Kuyper once said, "There is not a square inch in the whole domain

---

1. Andrew Christofides, *The Life Sentence* (Milton Keynes, UK: Paternoster Press, 2002), 11.

2. Christofides, *The Life Sentence*, 13.

of our human existence over which Christ, who is Sovereign over all, does not cry: 'Mine!'"³ He directs everything in your life—the family into which you were born, the church you attend, the friends who have crossed your path, the fact that you are reading this book now. God has ordained all these things. It should make you tremble to think that out of the twenty billion people who have ever lived, including the eight billion people living right now, the God of heaven and earth is reaching out to you!

God is *omnipresent*—He is everywhere (Ps. 139:7–8)—and *omniscient*—He knows everything (Ps. 139:1–4). That He sees everything is both a frightening and comforting thought. It's frightening because He knows everything about us. Nothing you or I have ever done, thought, or said has gone unnoticed. Every shameful secret we've hidden; every lustful thought we've had; every sinful website we have visited; every spiteful thing we've said—He's seen it all.

So, how can this possibly be a comforting thought? It's comforting because despite all the things God knows about you, He still invites you to come to Him. I'm sure your friends, family, girlfriend, and classmates like you at the moment, but if they knew what you were really like, they would probably feel differently. In fact, if everything about you came to light, people might be so disgusted that they would want to spit in your face! There are certain things we would hate others to know about us. Arthur Conan Doyle, who wrote the Sherlock Holmes stories, allegedly sent an anonymous note to lots of

---

3. Abraham Kuyper, "Sphere Sovereignty," in *Abraham Kuyper: A Centennial Reader*, ed. James D. Bratt (Grand Rapids: Eerdmans, 1998), 488.

famous people in Britain. The note read, "Flee! All has been discovered," and many of them left the country. Can I tell you the same? All has been discovered *about you*—but the One who has discovered these things is the same One who offers to forgive you for everything you've done. There's nothing He doesn't know about you that will change His mind. He knows you better than you know yourself, and yet He still says, "Come to Me" (Matt. 11:28).

God is *holy*. Scripture emphasizes this attribute most because it touches all the others (Pss. 99:9; 111:9; Rev. 15:4). Holiness is the very beauty of God. Holiness is what sets God apart from us. We may properly say that every facet of God's nature and every aspect of His character is holy. Most central, however, is God's purity, which cannot tolerate any form of sin (Hab. 1:13).

God is *majestic*. When John saw the Son of God in all His glory, he fell at His feet as if he were dead (Rev. 1:17). This tells us a lot about true Christian worship. God is awesome, and when people come into His presence, they tremble. Today, many church services are too relaxed, and people casually approach God—this is alien to biblical Christianity.

But even though God is holy and majestic, He is also *merciful* and *gracious*. Mercy means that He doesn't treat us as we deserve. Grace means that He shows kindness toward us that we do not deserve. Indeed, our God will abundantly pardon (Isa. 55:7). Perhaps the best picture of this mercy and grace is found in the Parable of the Lost Son (Luke 15:11–32). The younger son moved far away from home, as far away from his father as possible, but not before getting his share of the inheritance. He spent all the money on partying, prostitutes, and riotous living, but then a famine struck. He suddenly had no money and no friends, just a pigsty and the swine's leftover food. He decides to go back to his father and apologize—perhaps his father will hire him as one of his workers. But the story says that while he was still a long way off, a dot in the distance, his father spots him (no doubt he'd been looking out for him every day he was away) and runs to meet him. In that culture, distinguished patriarchs ordinarily did not run. Children did, women were known to, young men might, but not dignified pillars of the community. In this parable, though, God is pictured picking up His robe, baring His legs like some young boy, and sprinting. He then pounces on His son in love, not only before he has a chance to clean up his life but also before he can even recite his repentance speech. And the same God, who is now in heaven, will pick up His robe and run to all His children who call out to Him, however much of a mess they are in. He will also come to anyone who calls out to Him for the first time.

God is *good* (Ps. 86:5). There is nothing bad about Him. And He is our *Father*—a good father, a father who will never let us down or desert us. In Isaiah 9:6, one of the names given to the Lord Jesus is "Everlasting Father." This is not a reference to the eternal nature of His person but to the never-ending care of His fatherhood. He is a father forever.

God is *unchangeable* (Mal. 3:6; James 1:17). He is not temperamental. He does not show mercy with a grudge—His mercies are *tender*. One time, my parents' car broke down in Cardiff, and they called me to go and help them. I was up to my eyes in work. I went to help them, but, boy, did I do it grudgingly! I let my parents know how busy I was and really huffed at them. Thankfully, God is nothing like me. He delights to show mercy time and time again. He has never huffed at me.

God is seen most clearly in the face of *Jesus Christ*. The Lord Jesus said, "He who has seen Me has seen the Father" (John 14:9). An Indian philosopher, while explaining the difference between Islam and Christianity, said that Allah was too majestic to lie in a dirty manger, hang on a shameful cross, and enter filthy hearts. His adherents have to get to him. But the Bible says: look in that manger, survey that cross, and behold your God!

8

TRUST

Of all the actions young men must fulfill, the most important is to *trust*. Trust the Lord Jesus Christ completely.

Your Soul

Trust Jesus to save you. Don't rely on anything or anyone else. Trust really means taking God at His word. It means believing what He has done and what He has promised. You have to know certain things and believe them to be true: that you are a sinner in need of salvation, that you cannot save yourself, and that Jesus Christ is the Son of God and the only Savior. You then have to entrust your whole life to Him. Throw your whole self upon Him—your past, your present, and your future. Stop trusting yourself and trust Him. Your acceptance with God is completely dependent on Jesus Christ. Do not rely on your efforts and good works, but rest completely in what Jesus accomplished on the cross of Calvary.

Your Life

Entrust your whole life to God. Entrust your future to Him, and trust Him to guide you. He knows what is best for us.

Today, people have so many things to worry about: the future, exams, relationships, money, mortgages, marriages, children, grandchildren. Why not bring all these cares to the "Ancient of Days" (Dan. 7:9)? Trust Him to guide you even when the way is difficult and confusing. Trust His Word even when it opposes modern thinking and your desires. He knows what is best. This means we can remain patient when things seem to go against us (Genesis 37; 39–48; 50).

The evidence that you really trust God is that you trust Him in, and for, everything. You trust Him to guide you through life, in the good times and the bad. You trust that He is sovereign and that all things work together for your good (Rom. 8:28). Even when it doesn't make sense, even when it flies in the face of public opinion, you still trust Him and believe that He knows best. Proverbs tells us to "Trust in the LORD with all your heart, and lean not on your own understanding; in all your ways acknowledge Him, and He shall direct your paths" (Prov. 3:5–6). Olyott writes,

> Our heavenly Father is good and has no intention of misleading any of His children. Those who feed their minds on His Word, patiently wait on Him in prayer and sincerely desire to spend their lives pleasing Him, will not be left in the dark about which way He wants them to go.[1]

---

1. Stuart Olyott, *Something Must Be Known and Felt: A Missing Note in Today's Christianity* (Bridgend, UK: Bryntirion Press, 2014), 112.

Given what we discovered in chapter 7 about the character of God—that He is all powerful, sovereign, good, and wise—we should not seek to advise Him, correct Him, question Him, or counsel Him in our prayers. Simply lay your worries at His feet, and then trust Him.

9

REPENT

Today's action is to *repent*. If you have faith in Jesus Christ and totally trust in Him, then you will repent—that is, you will turn away from your sin and your old way of life. Your views, values, goals, and behaviors will all change, and you will live your whole life differently. Indeed, repentance means living a *new* life. You never want to sin, and when you do, you hate it. As William Gurnall said, repentance is "to forsake sin…to leave it without any thought reserved of returning to it again."[1]

Repentance is very different from regret. Writing to the Corinthians, Paul talks about worldly sorrow that doesn't change a person, sorrow that is simply the consequence of sin (2 Cor. 7:10). This kind of sorrow does not constitute true repentance for how our sin grieves God and violates our relationship with Him. As soon as the consequences go away, the behavior comes back. Regret is all about us. Repentance is all about God and how He feels.

---

1. Quoted in I. D. E. Thomas, comp., *The Golden Treasury of Puritan Quotations* (Edinburgh: Banner of Truth, 2000), 281.

If you are not a Christian, why not turn from your sin to Jesus Christ? Find a room where you can be alone and shut the door. Don't pretend to be someone you are not. Own up to who you are. Pray to God and say with the hymnist,

> Nothing in my hands I bring,
> Simply to Thy cross I cling;…
> Foul, I to the fountain fly,
> Wash me, Savior, or I die.[2]

But repentance is not something we do once—Christians have to repent every day.

---

2. Augustus Toplady, "Rock of Ages," 1776.

10

COMMUNE

In chapter 7, we discovered God's character. Today's action is to *commune* with God Himself. To commune means to get very close to someone by exchanging feelings or thoughts. Amazingly, we can come to know this great God intimately. We can know the Lord Jesus as a person just as well as we know other people—wives, families, friends, colleagues, neighbors, and so on. As A. W. Tozer wrote, "A loving personality dominates the Bible…men can know God with at least the same degree of immediacy as they know any other person or thing that comes within the field of their experience."[1] The more we get to know Him and commune with Him, the more we will become like Him.

Friends with God

In Exodus 33:11, we are told that God talked to Moses as a friend. In Isaiah 41:8, God calls Abraham His friend, while Genesis 18 describes the Son of God in a preincarnate state (known as a theophany), eating at the table of Abraham, His

---

1. A. W. Tozer, *The Pursuit of God* (London: Marshall, Morgan & Scott, 1961), 50–51.

friend. Nearly two thousand years later, this same Son of God became a man, Jesus of Nazareth, and dwelt among men and women, eating and drinking with them.

The Holy Spirit

Just before He ascended to heaven, Jesus told His disciples that, although He was leaving them physically, He wasn't truly leaving them—He would send the Holy Spirit (Acts 1:4–8). Through His Spirit, they (and us) can enjoy His presence morning, noon, and night. Before, the Lord Jesus could only be in one place at a time—now, He can be with His people everywhere, all the time.

Through the Holy Spirit, we can enjoy God's presence today. The Bible teaches plainly that all Christians have the Holy Spirit within them. Indeed, you cannot be a Christian unless the Holy Spirit is at work in your heart. He convicts you of sin, grants you the faith to believe, strengthens you to overcome temptation, deepens your love for God, and produces the fruit of the Spirit in your life—love, joy, peace, patience, kindness, goodness, faithfulness, gentleness, and self-control (Gal. 5:22–23).

Moreover, the Lord Jesus said, "where two or three are gathered together in My name, I am there in the midst of them" (Matt. 18:20). Every time Christians meet, even just two of them, Jesus is there with them as much as they are there with each other.

The presence of God is not only a doctrine to believe but also an experience to enjoy. Christianity affects the emotions. It is something that must be known and felt. In 2 Timothy

4:17, the apostle Paul says he felt the presence of Christ as he defended himself against Emperor Nero. But how can we, too, feel His presence?

The Bible

As a rule, the Lord Jesus presents Himself through the Bible. He will make the Bible alive as we read it and hear it preached. At times, this will even cause our hearts to burn (Luke 24:32). We really get to know God through the Bible. In fact, the whole reason we read our Bible is to get to know Christ better and better and better, to fall in love with the God of the Bible. The ones who find God are those who diligently seek Him (Heb. 11:6), who seek Him with all their hearts (Jer. 29:13). He wants to know that you are serious about Him. We should make this our goal as we read our Bible and hear it preached. May our eyes be open to the fact that the Almighty God is speaking to us, and may we see Him in all His love, glory, beauty, and majesty. He will then become precious to us (1 Peter 2:7).

Holiness

We will not feel God's presence if we live in a way that grieves Him. Flee from sin, and Jesus will draw near. As John writes, "God is light and in Him is no darkness at all" (1 John 1:5). This makes fellowship between God and unholy men impossible, such that the pursuit of holiness and righteousness must be a central concern for Christians (2 Cor. 6:14–7:1; Heb. 12:10–17; 1 John 1:5–2:1). Because God is holy, God's people must be holy too (Isa. 6:5). We pursue holiness by obeying God's Word. If we love God, we will keep His commandments

(John 14:15). The Lord Jesus Christ says, "As the Father loved Me, I also have loved you; abide in My love. If you keep My commandments, you will abide in My love, just as I have kept My Father's commandments and abide in His love" (John 15:9–10). We have communion with God by keeping His commandments, not because we have to but because we want to please Him, not out of duty but out of love. His commandments do not spoil our fun and burden us (1 John 5:3)—they bring us into close communion with God. They are beautiful. Read them (Exodus 20) and imagine how happy we would all be if we kept them.

God's People and Sufferings
We also get to know God by communing with God's people and by suffering. Suffering drives us to seek Him more in prayer, through which He draws close to us. As Samuel Rutherford would say when facing trials, "Here comes my Jesus."

II

READ

Having been in education for the last twenty-five years or so, I realize that most boys are not naturally inclined to read—but it is vital that young Christian men read. And if reading in general is hard, then reading the Bible is even harder! But, as the little Sunday school song says, "Read your Bible and pray every day if you want to grow" (see 2 Tim. 3:14–17; 1 Peter 2:2; 3:18). This is the best, simplest advice anyone can give you. As the saying goes, "The appetite grows with the eating."

Use Bible-reading plans to help you. Robert Murray M'Cheyne's is one of the best. Or use the book *Search the Scriptures*.[1] I have also found SPECK helpful:

- S – Is there a Sin the passage is telling me to kill?
- P – Is there a Promise I can claim?
- E – Is there an Example to follow?
- C – Is there a Command to obey?
- K – How does the passage increase my Knowledge of the triune God?

---

1. See Alan M. Stibbs, ed., *Search the Scriptures: A Three-Year Daily Devotional Guide to the Whole Bible* (Downers Grove, Ill.: InterVarsity Press, 2004).

In addition to the Bible, read good books. They will genuinely change your life. Read a mixture of Christian books: commentaries, to understand the Bible better; doctrine, to learn what Christians believe; church history, biographies, and devotional books, to be encouraged to know and love God more; and books about issues that Christians face today. The appendix at the back of this book is a suggested reading list. It is not exhaustive, but it includes different types of books that will introduce you to some of the Christian classics. It is designed for young people to read good Christian books over a four-year period. It is meant to supplement reading the whole Bible alongside *Search the Scriptures*. You can dip in and out of the reading program, or even follow it at your own pace. The reading list comprises a target to aim for, not a minimum requirement for participation. Just try to read as many of the books each year as you can. If nine is too many, shoot for five a year, or even three.

12

THINK

Reading is important, but it's not enough. Finishing your daily Bible reading as quickly as possible—like it is some burdensome chore standing between you and the rest of your day—simply won't cut it. Indeed, reading the Bible should not be seen as something that Christians *have* to do. Rather, it's an opportunity to hear what God has to say. The Bible is the Word of God, a living book. A church elder once told me, "Lift your Bible to your nose, and you will smell God's breath!"

To really benefit from the Scriptures, we need to *think* about, or meditate on, what we are reading. The psalmist writes, "Blessed is the man who walks not in the counsel of the ungodly, nor stands in the path of sinners, nor sits in the seat of the scornful; but his delight is in the law of the LORD, and in His law he meditates day and night" (Ps. 1:1–2). We need to truly meditate on the Bible and let it change the way we think and act (Josh. 1:8; Ps. 119:11; Rom. 12:2).

It may be helpful to think of your Bible as your hand. It has four fingers: Read, Study, Listen, and Memorize. It also has a thumb, the most important, which is Meditate. The Hebrew word for meditate means "mumble." As you read the Scriptures, mumble to yourself—have a conversation with your Bible. It is a living book, the Word of God, so as you read it, picture God speaking to you. Ask questions and really think about what it says. Grow to love your Bible and let it transform you.

13

PRAY

The Lord Jesus said that men ought always to pray (Luke 18:1). Prayer is evidence that a person is a Christian. The sign that Paul had become a Christian was that he prayed (Acts 9:11). James Montgomery, in one of his hymns, writes that prayer is "the Christian's vital breath."[1] But in my experience, and that of many other Christians, praying is one of the hardest things to do. We have to work at it, cultivate it, make it a habit.

Refreshing

There is a right and wrong way to pray. There are prayers that God will hear and prayers that He won't. We must, therefore, have a right view of prayer. So many people think that prayer is all about them—you ask for what you want, and you get it—whereas the Lord Jesus clearly thought prayer was refreshing. He had no sins to confess like we do. He didn't see prayer as a bargaining chip but, rather, as a time to spend with His Father. Amid all His circumstances, many of them difficult, He often withdrew from the crowds to talk with His Father. This is how

---

1. James Montgomery, "Prayer Is the Soul's Sincere Desire," 1818.

we should see prayer: precious time spent with God, in which we can simply enjoy His company. We can ask Him to draw near to us, tell Him about our day, adore His majesty, explain to Him our temptations, and ask Him to forgive us all our sins. Viewing prayer like this will be so refreshing. It shouldn't be just another duty—it should be the highlight of the day. As a Christian, I can spend time alone, as often as I want, with the God of heaven and earth!

Reverence

When we pray, we need to know whom we are approaching. He is God, so we need to come reverently. As the apostle Paul approached God, he said, "I bow my knees" (Eph. 3:14). Throughout the Bible, there are so many examples of people praying reverently (2 Chron. 6:13; 7:3; 29:20, 29; Ezra 9:5; Neh. 8:6; Pss. 5:7; 132:7; 138:2; Isa. 45:23; Acts 7:60; 20:36; 21:5; Rom. 14:11; Phil. 2:10). The best example occurs in the garden of Gethsemane, where it would seem that Jesus knelt as He prayed (Luke 22:41). I don't think that this one verse requires us to pray in a kneeling position. However, it tells us a lot. If the sinless, perfect Son of God knelt to pray, then I cannot come into the presence of a holy God just any old way. I need to remember exactly who I am and who He is. I am a sinner entering the presence of a holy God—I must come with reverence and awe.

Intimacy

We must also approach God intimately. Again in the garden of Gethsemane, the Lord Jesus's prayer was intimate. He was coming to His Father. This is the only time in the Gospels where Jesus addresses the Father with the personal pronoun, "My Father" (Matt. 26:39). He cries out, "Abba, Father" (Mark 14:36). This is as intimate as saying, "Dad." By faith in Jesus, His Father is our Father, and we, too, can enjoy this intimate relationship. Jesus tells Christians not to think of God as our creator or our judge first, but as our Father. He didn't teach us to pray, "Our Creator in heaven," or "Our Judge in heaven," but "Our Father in heaven" (Matt. 6:9).

Prayer is such a privilege. To think that people like us can have an audience with the living God, who loves to hear our prayers. John writes, "there was silence in heaven for about half an hour" (Rev. 8:1). It would seem that this silence occurs because prayers are being offered up to heaven—if so, this is a view of prayer from the vantage point of heaven. We may think that our prayers are pointless. We may have sat through dry, boring prayer meetings in which our prayers appear to go unanswered. But there may have been silence in heaven because God's people on earth are crying out to Him. True prayer ascends to the very throne of God (Rev. 8:3–5). It is as if God says, "hush—My people are praying." He stills heaven, as it were, to listen to the prayers of His people. Indeed, prayer lies at the very center of His relationship with His people. In 1 Samuel 1, the prayers of a relatively obscure woman in the hill country of Ephraim matter to Yahweh of hosts, cosmic Ruler, Sovereign of every and all power. He listens to and answers her prayers as she laid her distress at His feet. Through prayer, God makes us participants in His governance over the world. And when we pray, the Holy Spirit helps us—He enters into the task with us (Rom. 8:26–27).

Wrestle

I urge you, young men, to devote yourselves to prayer and truly grapple with God through it. Like Jacob, wrestle with God in prayer (Gen. 32:22–32). Real prayer is not letting Him go until He blesses us. We tell God everything we have on our hearts. Find a room where you can be alone and shut the door. Sit quietly until your whole being is still. Don't hurry. Tell the Lord everything. According to Olyott,

> we pray ourselves empty. We go over it and over it again and again until we have nothing else to say. We hold nothing back. With tears we have confessed every sin we know about and all our foolishness. We have told Him every mistake, every worry, every fear, every ache and pain, every difficulty we face.[2]

Prayer Meeting

Besides praying on your own, attend the weekly prayer meeting at your church and pray with other Christians. If your church doesn't have a weekly prayer meeting, leave and find one that does! The prayer meeting is the most important meeting of all—indeed, some call it the engine room of the church. You often hear Christians say that they are "praying for the work," but the truth is, prayer is the real work. In Acts 6:4, the apostles say, "we will give ourselves continually

---

2. Olyott, *Something Must Be Known and Felt*, 135.

to prayer." When the Israelites were at war with the Amalekites, Moses did the most extraordinary thing a leader can do: he left the battlefield and put young Joshua in charge. With Aaron and Hur, he climbed the nearest hill and lifted up his hands in prayer to God. When Moses kept his hands raised, Israel prevailed, and when Moses let down his hands, Amalek prevailed. The front line of the battle, they discovered, was not on the field but on the mountaintop (Ex. 17:8–15). The strength of a church can be measured by its prayer meeting.

Intercession

Don't worry about how your prayers sound. Remember—at God's right hand is the Lord Jesus Christ, who intercedes for us and makes our prayers acceptable to God (Rom. 8:34). A minister once came to preach at the Heath Evangelical Church in Cardiff and illustrated this well. He said that his niece came in from the garden, where she had picked flowers for her mother. What the little girl actually had in her hand was a clump of earth with some flowers mixed up with weeds. Her sentiment was lovely, in that she wanted to bring something nice for her mother. The minister said he spent time with the little girl picking out the weeds and getting rid of the earth to make the flowers a presentable posy for her mother. That is a picture of what Jesus Christ does with our prayers. We come to God in prayer, and our theology is not always correct. We stumble and stammer, repeating ourselves and not really saying what we want to. But in heaven, there's a man, the God-man Jesus Christ, who intercedes on our behalf. Spurgeon said, "I thank God my prayers go to heaven in the revised version."

Practical Tips

Regarding practical tips for prayer, I have found "ACTS" helpful: Adoration, Confession, Thanksgiving, and Supplication. Adoration is when I worship God for who He is and adore His attributes. Maybe focus on one each day. I confess my sins to God and ask Him to forgive them. I thank God, considering all the things for which I can be thankful that day. And then I make supplication. I make my requests known to God.

There are some things that He will not grant, especially that which is expressly against His Word. I cannot pray to rob a bank and get away with it! There are other things that He has promised to grant. "If we confess our sins, He is faithful and just to forgive us our sins" (1 John 1:9). Take those promises and pray them back to God. There are still more things that He hasn't promised or forbade, for which I can ask Him. If He doesn't give me these things, I trust that He knows best. According to Calvin, "Nothing is adapted better to excite us to prayer than a full conviction that we shall be heard."[3] But, as Olyott wrote, "It is foolish to pray against sin and then to sin against prayer."[4]

---

3. John Calvin, *Commentary on a Harmony of the Evangelists, Matthew, Mark, and Luke* (Edinburgh: Calvin Translation Society, 1845), 1:351.

4. Olyott, *Something Must Be Known and Felt*, 91.

14

DENY

Of all the actions we are called to do, the hardest is certainly to *deny*. Underneath every other excuse, it is without doubt the reason why people refuse to become Christians.

The Lord Jesus Christ was not a salesman who just told people what they wanted to hear. He said that anyone who wanted to be saved would have to lose his life: "If anyone desires to come after Me, let him deny himself, and take up his cross, and follow Me. For whoever desires to save his life will lose it, but whoever loses his life for My sake will find it" (Matt. 16:24–25).

To become a Christian is to take up your cross daily and follow Jesus Christ—it is to die to self every day. Christians no longer live for themselves, but now submit their lives to the Lord Jesus. This is the hardest thing in the world for anyone to do. We all love ourselves; we want to please ourselves, and we don't want to deny ourselves anything. But let me ask you this: Has living for yourself made you happy? Are you satisfied and content? The actor Jim Carrey once said, "I think everybody should get rich and famous and do everything they ever dreamed of so they can see that it's not the answer."[1] If you gained the whole world, it would not make you happy.

Jesus Christ is kind. He is not out to make you unhappy or to deny you things for the sake of it. He made us, and He knows what is best for us. The things He tells us in the Bible not to do, and the things He commands us to do, are all for our good. It is for our good that we read the Bible and submit ourselves to what it says. Living for myself, thinking about myself, worrying about myself, trying to please myself—all of this leads to exhaustion, discontent, and failure. The hardest thing to do is to deny "me." I love me. I live for me. It is all about me. But, at the same time, "me" is my biggest problem. I am a slave to my lusts. I am insecure. I struggle to keep up with my job. I am tired of following the latest trend. My personality sometimes gets on my nerves. Oh, to be free from being me! Embracing the world has made me weary and heavy laden. But Jesus invites us to come to Him. If we put His yoke upon us and learn from Him, He will give us rest (Matt. 11:28). Whoever loses his life for Christ's sake will keep it, but whoever tries to save his life will lose it (Luke 17:33). By living for Jesus, we find true peace and happiness.

Like Moses, we must count the cost. He was a prince in Egypt but gave it all up. He refused to be called the son of Pharaoh's daughter, choosing rather to be mistreated with the people of God than to enjoy the fleeting pleasures of sin. He considered the reproach of Christ greater wealth than the treasures of Egypt, for he was looking to the reward. By faith

---

1. Jay Stone, "Carrey's Been Busted," *Ottawa Citizen*, December 16, 2005.

he left Egypt, unafraid of Pharaoh's anger, for he endured as seeing Him who is invisible (Heb. 11:24–27). In the same vein, the apostle Paul writes, "I also count all things loss for the excellence of the knowledge of Christ Jesus my Lord, for whom I have suffered the loss of all things, and count them as rubbish, that I may gain Christ" (Phil. 3:8).

15

KILL

....

Today's action, *kill*, sounds drastic. That's because it is. Christians are called to kill sin, to take drastic action against it (Rom. 8:13). People often think of "sin" as a list of things they shouldn't do. But sin is more than that—it's a power that destroys us. At first, sin seems fun and pleasurable, but it can take hold of us and ruin our lives (Col. 1:13; Heb. 2:15). Sin is a dangerous, controlling power. Every sinful action is one step toward a habit, and then an addiction.

A young man sits in his room alone with his computer and thinks he'll click on an image just once. Before he knows it, he's addicted to pornography. The first time the alcoholic got drunk, he didn't plan to become addicted. Sin destroys lives and causes much suffering. It troubles your conscience and wracks you with guilt. It leaves you feeling dirty. Like an addict, you won't think straight until you get a hit of your particular sin. That is why we must kill sin. If we don't kill sin, sin will kill us.

There may be a particular sin with which you really struggle or a relationship that you just can't give up. Maybe, probably, it is a sexual sin. When sex is involved, most men stop thinking straight. Lust, pornography, adultery, fornication—these are all things men think they can control, but they end up *being* controlled. Every time you indulge in sexual sin, you think it will be the last time, but you keep going back for more. However, sex is not the only thing that overpowers and enslaves us. Any number of sins can do this: hatred, jealousy, anger, selfish ambition, drunkenness, and greed, to name a few.

God hates sin, and if we continue sinning, it will take us to hell. We must not feed our temptations and succumb to sin. Rather, we must weed out sin. Putting sin to death is not easy. It is hard work and requires all our energy. We have a big garden in London, which sounds great, but it is such hard work to keep it looking nice. We don't simply mow the lawn, pull the weeds, and trim the bushes once—we have to stay on top of it all the time. Likewise, we have to kill sin daily. In order to do that, we must know ourselves, including our particular weaknesses, and then do whatever it takes to put our sins to death. Avoid watching certain types of films, going to certain places, and spending time with people who will lead you astray. Make yourself accountable to a good Christian friend and have him check your computer regularly. In short, do whatever it takes to kill sin.

It takes great effort and the help of the Holy Spirit to overcome. Be ruthless with sin. Ask yourself, "Is the sin I love so much worth eternal hellfire?" The Lord Jesus Christ said, "If your right eye causes you to sin, pluck it out and cast it from you; for it is more profitable for you that one of your members perish, than for your whole body to be cast into hell. And if your right hand causes you to sin, cut it off and cast it from you; for it is more profitable for you that one of your members perish, than for your whole body to be cast into hell" (Matt. 5:29–30).

Killing sin isn't just a negative action. We have to positively dedicate our lives to God (Rom. 6:12–19; Phil. 1:20). In other words, we can't just weed out sin—we must sow righteousness. In 1 Timothy 6:11, the apostle Paul writes, "But you, O man of God, flee these things and pursue righteousness, godliness, faith, love, patience, gentleness." We need to cultivate new habits and fill the void left by our dead sins through abiding in the Lord Jesus Christ (John 15). This means keeping His commandments, meditating on His Word, worshiping Him with His people, praying to Him, and meeting around His table.

Moreover, the Devil makes work for idle hands, so we need to be busy doing good works and having good clean fun. When you submit yourself to God and resist the Devil, James writes that "he will flee from you" (James 4:7). As the old hymn says,

> Yield not to temptation,
> For yielding is sin;
> Each vict'ry will help you,
> Some other to win;
> Fight valiantly onward,
> Evil passions subdue;
> Look ever to Jesus,
> He will carry you through.

> Refrain:
> Ask the Savior to help you,
> Comfort, strengthen and keep you;
> He is willing to aid you,
> He will carry you through.
>
> Shun evil companions,
> Bad language disdain;
> God's name hold in rev'rence,
> Nor take it in vain;
> Be thoughtful and earnest,
> Kindhearted and true;
> Look ever to Jesus,
> He will carry you through.
>
> To him that o'ercometh,
> God giveth a crown;
> Through faith we will conquer,
> Though often cast down;
> He who is our Savior,
> Our strength will renew;
> Look ever to Jesus,
> He will carry you through.[1]

We must approach sin in the way that Winston Churchill approached the Nazis after the evacuation from Dunkirk in 1940: "We shall fight on the beaches, we shall fight on the landing grounds, we shall fight in the fields and in the streets, we shall fight in the hills; we shall never surrender."

---

1. H. R. Palmer, "Yield Not to Temptation," 1868.

16

LIVE

Many people think that when a man becomes a Christian, he stops living. But the opposite is true. John writes his gospel so that "you may believe that Jesus is the Christ, the Son of God, and that believing you may have life" (John 20:31). When we become Christians, the life of God—new life—is put into our souls. The Bible says that we pass from death to life (John 5:25). Instead of being a slave to sin, we are now slaves to righteousness as we live for God (Rom. 6:17–18). We want to do what is right and pleasing to God. We walk in a new direction. We have new inclinations and new affections. Indeed, Christians are new creations (James 1:18). We have put off the old man and put on the new man (Col. 3:9–10). We go from darkness to light (Acts 26:18; Col. 1:13).

By faith, Christians are not fooled into thinking that sin will make them happy. There are so many examples of the deceitfulness and destructiveness of sin. Pubs and clubs are full of excitement on a Friday night, but by the end of the weekend, people have done all sorts of seemingly pleasurable things that have left them feeling guilty and, at worst, that have wrecked their marriages, families, and friendships. They wake up feeling empty, hating themselves and those with whom they've committed shameful acts. People grow infatuated with the pleasures of sin, but in the end, they loathe themselves. Sin promises so much but always leaves you feeling dirty and guilty. William Gurnall wrote, "Faith looks behind the curtain of sense, and sees sin before it is dressed up for the stage," while Joel Beeke says, "Faith sees the ugliness and hellishness of sin without its camouflage."

But even the best things in this life will not satisfy our deepest longings. Today, young men chase after fame, power, body image, money, sports, and sex, believing that these things will fulfill us—but they won't. As the Rolling Stones sang, we "can't get no satisfaction." The best the world can offer, and the biggest achievements we can possibly attain, fail to fulfill our deepest needs. Jonny Wilkinson proved this point when he described what it was like to win the Rugby World Cup for England. It was the pinnacle of his career, something almost every schoolboy in the country dreams of. But this is what he said:

> I had already begun to feel the elation slipping away from me during the lap of honour around the field. I couldn't believe that all the effort was losing its worth so soon. This was something I had fantasised about achieving since I was a child. In my head I had reached the peak of the mountain and now all that was left was to slowly descend the other side. I'd just achieved my greatest ambition and it felt a bit empty.[1]

---

1. Jonny Wilkinson, "Jonny Wilkinson: Winning Has Its Drawbacks," *The Times*, November 21, 2009, https://www.thetimes.co.uk/article/jonny-wilkinson-winning-has-its-drawbacks-g2jwn22p72c.

The foundation of a Christian's joy is that all his sins have been forgiven. Instead of feeling empty and restless, uneasy and guilty, he can know contentment, peace, and happiness—a deep-seated joy that is independent of his circumstances. God, the Creator of heaven and earth, who holds the whole universe in His hand, is the Christian's loving Father. Of course, believers are not immune from trials and grief, but they can rest in the knowledge that all things work together for their good (Rom. 8:28). No matter what they go through, the Lord Jesus will never leave them nor forsake them (Heb. 13:5) and has promised to be with them always (Matt. 28:20). They also have the hope of heaven to anticipate.

Why, then, are so many Christians unhappy? As he expresses in Psalm 51, David had lost his joy because he had sinned and strayed from God (Ps. 51:12). When we try to keep one foot in the world and one foot in the church, we will never know true happiness. We have to be out and out for the Lord Jesus Christ—we have to give our whole lives to Him.

In John 10:10, the Lord Jesus says, "The thief does not come except to steal, and to kill, and to destroy. I have come that they may have life, and that they may have it more abundantly." God has given us so many good things to enjoy: music, food, laughter, friendship, love, family, travel, sports, art, and more. He is not out to spoil our fun or make us miserable. Christians should enjoy these good gifts from God (Eccl. 3:12–13; James 1:17), but they must not let their happiness depend on these things—rather, they must put God first. "But seek first the kingdom of God and His righteousness, and all these things shall be added to you" (Matt. 6:33). If you do this, you will begin to *live* life in all its fullness, to the glory of God.

17

WORK

It is imperative that young Christian men *work* hard. Do not be lazy (Rom. 12:11). Today, many seem to believe that laziness is cool, that indifference is funny, that getting rich quick is the goal, and that, somehow, all this is manly. But God made it very clear in Genesis 2:15 that everyone has to work hard. Even before sin entered the world (Genesis 3), Adam was not meant to live a life of pleasant idleness in the garden of Eden—he was to tend and keep it. Work is good for us, physically and mentally. We find it so difficult, exhausting, and stressful because of the fall.

Work for the Lord
Christians in schools, colleges, and universities may not be the brightest students, but they should be the most diligent. Do not just work hard to gain recognition or to please someone who is watching (Eph. 6:6). Remember: you ultimately serve the Lord Jesus Christ (Col. 3:24). This is particularly helpful if you have a teacher or a professor whom you dislike, or if you work for a boss who is unkind to you. Even in those situations, you should be polite and respectful (Titus 2:9–10;

1 Peter 2:18–20). Always be reliable and punctual. Maybe your work is boring, hard, and monotonous, but approaching it as if you were serving the Lord will transform your attitude (1 Cor. 10:31).

As a student or an employee, you must be faithful and obedient (Eph. 6:5). If you become a boss one day—perhaps you already are a boss—be sure to deal with your employees fairly. Treat them kindly; never bully them. Pay them what they deserve and do not defraud them (Lev. 19:13; Deut. 24:14; Amos 5:8–13; Luke 10:7; Col. 4:1; James 5:4). Make sure your job does not and will not cause you to undermine scriptural teaching. Don't work on Sundays unless it is a necessity (Ex. 34:21). And while it is important to work hard, do not make work your god.

Use Your God-Given Talents

It is also important to do a job for which you are physically and intellectually capable—that is, a job where you can use your God-given talents and abilities. In modern education, young people are told that they can do anything if they put their mind to it. They just need to believe and have the right attitude. Then they go into a science lesson and learn that they are nothing more than a piece of slime on a blue planet! The Bible's teaching is completely different. It says that we are all fearfully and wonderfully made (Ps. 139:14) in the image of God (Gen. 1:27), but that sin has ruined us. We must bring our brokenness to God and ask Him to save us, cleanse us, and make us new creatures. Then, we are to use the specific talents and abilities God has given us for His glory. Some will be brilliant doctors, while others will sweep the streets, keeping our towns and cities clean. Don't waste your talent (Matt. 25:14–30) or envy someone else's talent. God has made you just the way He wants you to be.

Fit and Healthy

As you work hard in your school, college, university, or job, you must also work hard to keep fit and healthy. Eat well and exercise. The Lord Jesus must have been in shape. He had a lot of energy and endurance, which enabled Him to travel on foot for long journeys, preach for hours, and endure the sufferings of His final night and day. He didn't idolize His body, but He looked after it. Paul writes that bodily training is of some value (1 Tim. 4:8). There is a significant link between mental health and physical exercise. Our bodies are temples of the Holy Spirit, so we must glorify God in the way we treat our bodies (1 Cor. 6:19–20).

Work Out Your Salvation

We are also called to work out our salvation (Phil. 2:12). While the Bible teaches clearly that we are not saved because of our good works (Eph. 2:8), it also teaches that we are saved "for good works" (Eph. 2:10). In other words, we have to work at being a Christian. We must become more and more like the Lord Jesus Christ, knowing all the while that the work we do is enabled by the Holy Spirit working in us. This process is known as sanctification, and the Lord Jesus Christ died as much to sanctify us as He did to justify us (John 17:19; Eph. 5:26; Col. 1:22; Titus 2:14; 1 Peter 2:24). The way we know that we have been justified (made right with God) is that we are being sanctified (made holy). Sanctification is an ongoing transformation that produces righteousness in us. This happens when we read our Bibles (John 17:17), pray that God will sanctify us (Ps. 51:10), ask God's Spirit to help us (2 Thess. 2:13), attend church consistently, submit ourselves to the preaching of the Word of God, fellowship with Christians (Prov. 13:20), partake of the Lord's Supper regularly, and kill sin.

18

REST

The Sabbath, or the Lord's Day, is a contentious issue today. So, let's be clear: the Sabbath is important. God created the world with a Sabbath pattern (Gen. 2:3). The last command given to Moses before he came down from Mount Sinai was to "keep the Sabbath, therefore, for it is holy to you" (Ex. 31:14). And in the New Testament, Jesus upheld the Sabbath.

It is fitting and biblical, then, for one day in seven to be set aside for worship (Lev. 23:3; Luke 4:16; Acts 13:42–44; 15:21; 17:2; 18:4). After the Lord Jesus rose from the dead on a Sunday, Christians moved the Sabbath from Saturday to Sunday (Acts 20:7; 1 Cor. 16:1–2)—therefore, this day of rest is called the Lord's Day (Rev. 1:10). At the heart of this day is worship and rest set apart from normal labors (Lev. 23:3). It is a weekly reminder that God is God, and that we are not. Sunday should be different from the rest of the week (Ex. 20:8).

Jesus emphasized the spiritual significance of the Sabbath. While He certainly kept all the Sabbath commandments, He did not hesitate to break the traditions and customs surrounding the day. For Jesus, the Sabbath was a day of freedom (Luke 13:10–17), a day for healing (Luke 14:1–6), and a day for doing good (Mark 3:1–6). In the same way, Sunday should not be a day of rules and regulations for a Christian. It should be the best, most enjoyable day of the week. We should keep the Lord's Day special, not because we want to follow the rules, but because we love God and want to spend the day worshiping Him, resting, fellowshipping, reading, and praying.

There is no list of dos and don'ts to keep the Lord's Day holy. We are no longer bound to observe the Jewish Sabbath in a particular way. We still need to obey the fourth commandment (Matt. 5:17), but we also need to see how Christ transformed it. According to Luther,

> if anywhere the day is made holy for the mere day's sake—if anywhere anyone sets up its observance on a Jewish foundation, then I order you to work on it, to ride on it, to dance on it, to feast on it, to do anything that shall remove this encroachment on Christian liberty.[1]

Sunday is for our good, and we ought to enjoy it. God made us with a need for rest. We trust in Christ enough to rest one day in seven. The Sabbath was made for man, not man for the Sabbath (Mark 2:23–28). But we don't just take a break from our work—we rest in Christ, meditate on Him, and enjoy Him.

If a Christian simply attends church in the morning and then spends the rest of the day doing whatever he wants, it says a lot about how much he loves God. If he would rather watch TV, play sports, or do work on Sunday—in other

---

1. D. A. Carson, ed., *From Sabbath to Lord's Day: A Biblical, Historical and Theological Investigation* (Eugene, Ore.: Wipf and Stock, 1999), 314.

words, what he does on a normal day—there is something wrong. The Sabbath should be a day that we spend communing with God's people, listening to preaching, reading good Christian books, enjoying time with family, and turning aside from earthly labor and recreation.

Calvin writes this about the Sabbath:

> It is extraordinary that God demands of our pride nothing more onerous than that we should observe his sabbath by resting from our labours. Yet there is nothing which we are more reluctant to do than to cease from all our works and to make room for his.[2]

---

2. John Calvin, *Institutes of the Christian Religion*, trans. Robert White (Edinburgh: Banner of Truth, 2014), 74.

19

SHINE

We live in a dark world. If you browse social media, watch the news, read the newspaper, or just attend school, college, or university, you will be bombarded by sadness, heartbreak, strife, crime, war, selfishness, and unkindness. In such a world, young Christian men are called to *shine*. You are the light of the world (Matt. 5:14–16), and you are to shine your light through your character and your actions.

Be kind. Don't revile people, exclude them, or gossip about them. Make an effort to talk to people, especially shy and awkward people whom others tend to avoid. Look out for the most vulnerable members of society. In my experience as a teacher over the last twenty-five years, there is nothing more admirable than boys who are kind, while there is nothing uglier than those who are spiteful, selfish, and abusive.

Be patient, even with those who are irritating, unlikable, and annoying. God often sends such people across our paths to make us more patient. The Lord Jesus was kind to the unloveliest of people and reached out to true social outcasts.

Be faithful, loyal, and trustworthy. Be self-controlled, however hard it may be. Don't be afraid to stand against the crowd and obey what the Bible says. Christians are most attractive to the world when they are different. Be good and clean. Don't complain and moan. Rather, be joyful and winsome.

Be meek, which is different from being weak. Meekness is strength under control. Don't flaunt your strength and power. Even though you could take advantage of a situation and capitalize on others' weaknesses, don't.

In other words, let your lives shine by bearing the fruit of the Spirit: "love, joy, peace, longsuffering, kindness, goodness, faithfulness, gentleness, self-control" (Gal. 5:22–23).

20

VIEW

Today's action is critical. When we neglect it, we invite unhappiness, failure, and stagnation. We need to *view* everything in the light of eternity: heaven and hell. We must realize that this world is just the shadowland. "We do not look at the things which are seen, but at the things which are not seen. For the things which are seen are temporary, but the things which are not seen are eternal" (2 Cor. 4:18).

People will spend eternity in one of two places: heaven or hell. We must live our lives in view of this. As the Puritan Thomas Watson admonished, we must "study eternity."

Hell

It is hard to take hell seriously. In the twenty-first century, even Bible-believing Christians have tried to sanitize hell and cover it up, as if it were an embarrassing family secret. But hell is as real and terrifying today as it always has been. Deep down, because of our inherent sense of justice, we all believe in hell. We think it is right when criminals go to prison, and we think it is unfair when the likes of Jimmy Savile appear to "get away with it." How much more should a holy God punish those who have sinned against Him. The Bible is clear: hell awaits everyone who is not saved.

Hell is a place no one wants to experience. But as you read this book, wherever you may be, there are people who once walked this earth, living and breathing like you, who now find themselves in hell. It is a place of outer darkness; a place where people gnash their teeth in pain and torment; a place where your conscience will trouble you forever. It is impossible to comprehend the horrors of hell—never hearing music ever again; never tasting good food ever again; never quenching your thirst ever again; never feeling loved ever again (Rev. 18:21–24). In short, absolute darkness and horrible loneliness. Everything we enjoy in this life—friendship, meals, a warm summer's evening, walks through the snow—is no longer ours to enjoy.

It is important to realize that God is in hell, but only in His anger. Those who end up in hell will spend eternity with the wrath of God hanging over them. And there is no escape; no fire exit; no prospect of getting out. As you read this book, imagine the people who have just arrived in hell. Think about their first five minutes there, their first hour; tomorrow, they will have endured their first day. Next week, they will have seen their first week; then, there's the first month to get through, and the first year. Picture their realization that this will last forever!

The most chilling words a person can hear are, "Depart from Me, you cursed, into the everlasting fire prepared for the devil and his angels" (Matt. 25:41). Those who hear this are banished to everlasting punishment (Matt. 25:46). Visualize it! Imagine it! Sent to hell forever!

Heaven
Heaven is a place of paradise. In heaven there will be no sin, no sorrow, no pain, no night, no death, and—especially relevant to our day—no stress (Rev. 21:4, 27; 22:5). My family and I were on vacation in West Wales a few years ago. It was a lovely spring evening. We were in the middle of nowhere, surrounded by beautiful scenery. It was totally peaceful. Then my wife said, as only my wife can, "Make the most of this. We'll be back at work and the real world next week, and the busyness of everyday life." But one day I will be in heaven, the real world, and my trip will be everlasting. I will never have to go back (Rev. 22:5).

Heaven is a place of breathtaking beauty. Seven-year-old Alice Scarlett Wakeling passed away peacefully on October 8, 2019, after battling a rare childhood cancer. Her obituary was published in *The Times*. She had become a Christian and spoke with her family until the very end, holding their hands. With her eyes closed, her last word was "wow." We cannot even imagine what that little girl saw, but one day, if you are a Christian, you will see it too.

Heaven is the eternal home of everyone who trusts in Jesus Christ. It is a house with many rooms (John 14:2). As our home, it is a place in which we are safe, relaxed, loved, cared for, welcomed, and wanted. There is no place like home—when we eventually enter heaven, God will, as it were, say to us, "Make yourself at home." Dwight L. Moody put it well:

Some day you will read in the papers that D. L. Moody, of East Northfield, is dead. Don't you believe a word of it! At that moment I shall be more alive than I am now. I shall have gone up higher, that is all.

Live your life in *view* of heaven and hell. As Colossians 3:2 says, "Set your mind on things above, not on things on the earth." Likewise, the Lord Jesus tells us in the Sermon on the Mount,

> Do not lay up for yourselves treasures on earth, where moth and rust destroy and where thieves break in and steal; but lay up for yourselves treasures in heaven, where neither moth nor rust destroys and where thieves do not break in and steal. For where your treasure is, there your heart will be also (Matt. 6:19–21).

21

STAND

Christians today are a minority group in a secular society. In some places, Christians are persecuted; in others, we are mocked, excluded, and pitied. Many believe Christian teaching is outdated, ridiculous, and offensive. In our "post-Christian," high-tech age, when a stiff cultural wind blows against the church, young men are called to *stand*. I cannot think of a better example to follow than Daniel.

In the book of Daniel, we are told that Jerusalem had been attacked as part of the Babylonian empire's expansion policy. The city fell in three stages, spanning the years 605, 597, and 587 BC (2 Kings 24:1–25:1). The siege described in Daniel 1 took place during the first of those stages, when King Nebuchadnezzar brought the cream of the crop to Babylon, the best young people Jerusalem had to offer. Daniel was one of these young men, and so this fourteen-year-old boy was taken five hundred miles east of Jerusalem, across the Syrian desert to Babylon, where he spent the next seventy years of his life and served under four kings.

Daniel lived far from home, as do Christians in every age. This world is not our home. Like Daniel, we are "sojourners and pilgrims" (1 Peter 2:11). But even though he was a long way from home, he stood firm. The Babylonian master plan was to reeducate these boys, transform their worldview, and brainwash them. The first step was to confuse their identity by changing their names (Dan. 1:6–7). Babylon also knew that reading shapes the mind, so the boys were made to learn its language and literature (1:4). So, here were these boys, many miles from home, isolated from their families and godly influences, being "Babylonized." They were to think like Babylonians, speak like Babylonians, eat like Babylonians, and drink like Babylonians.

We see the same approach today. The world—through what it teaches in schools and universities, on social media, on television, and in newspapers—seeks to isolate us from God's Word, indoctrinate us, confuse us, and make us compromise. But Daniel "purposed in his heart that he would not defile himself with the portion of the king's delicacies, nor with the wine which he drank" (Dan. 1:8). Daniel and his three friends took a stand over the change to their diet. The Jews had strict rules about food that were part of the ceremonial law. The ceremonial law was not fulfilled until Christ died on the cross. After that, no food was unclean—but at this time, many foods were unclean. Therefore, as far as Daniel was concerned, Babylon could relocate him, rename him, and reeducate him, but it could not make him disobey God's law. So, he drew the line.

Daniel asked Nebuchadnezzar's chief eunuch for permission to be excused from eating the king's food. The eunuch was frightened by this request, but Daniel didn't give up. He spoke to the steward, whom the chief eunuch had set over Daniel and his friends. In effect, Daniel said, "You put us to the test, and God will prove Himself." God showed them favor, and after three years of eating vegetables and drinking water,

> the king interviewed them, and among them all none was found like Daniel, Hananiah, Mishael, and Azariah; therefore they served before the king. And in all matters of wisdom and understanding about which the king examined them, he found them ten times better than all the magicians and astrologers who were in all his realm. (Dan. 1:19–20)

That Daniel and his friends looked so good despite their diet was a miracle. There was a snap to their skin—they looked vibrant and healthy.

Young Christian men today need to draw lines. You need to do all you can to get along with your classmates, teammates, and colleagues, but don't compromise your faith. Obey the Bible. Stand firm. Before you go off to university or start school, draw lines—things you will and will not do—and stick to them, however hard it may be and however much pressure you may feel.

It is quite likely that if our culture continues to decline, Christians will be persecuted. Ask yourself this question: "Will I stand if persecution comes?" The answer can be found by asking, "Am I standing now?" Daniel is probably most famous for being thrown in the lions' den (Daniel 6). But he won the battle of the lions' den not in chapter 6 but in chapter 1, when he drew his lines.

I once heard a story about a territorial army group that went on weekend maneuvers every six months. They stayed in barracks, and every time, one of the men would come back from the village pub half drunk on Saturday night. He would stagger into the dormitory around midnight and stand in the middle of the room. Then he would draw a line across the floor and shout to the other men, "I challenge any of you to cross this line!" He did this every six months for a few years, and the men would groan, roll over, and go back to sleep. But one of the newer soldiers had had enough of this. He got out of bed, walked up to the line, and crossed it. The drunk looked at him—he was a big, mean-looking fellow. The drunk hesitated, and then he took the chalk and drew another line further down. We have all seen Christians, churches, and organizations draw lines that they cravenly move when some "big man" comes along.

Like Daniel, stand. Don't roll over. And when you do stand, there will be consequences, but you will be joyful and content. It makes no sense, but it is the miracle of living for God.

22

TALK

Young men find it hard to *talk*, particularly about their feelings. They find it even harder to ask for help. But very often, the bravest word a young man can say is "help."

Apparently, young men worry about family issues, abuse, bereavement, relationships, academic pressure, peer pressure, self-worth, bullying, sexuality, substance abuse, anxiety, depression, and, worst of all, self-harm and suicide. Research shows that males are more likely to kill themselves than females. All of this underlines the importance of boys talking. It is okay to admit that we struggle with our emotions, and it is important to be honest about what we are going through. We live in a broken world (Rom. 8:18–19). Suffering is real, so we need to normalize talking about our emotions and problems, honestly and frankly. We can be honest about what we're going through. There is nothing "manly" about bottling things up.

To that end, it is important that young men have trustworthy Christian friends, other young men with whom they can be candid. Find young men who will help you; then, help them in return. Find friends who will hold you accountable, who will love you always, and who will help you through adversity (Prov. 17:17). In short, find a band of brothers (John 21:1–17). The best example of friendship in the Bible is probably that of David and Jonathan (1 Samuel 18–20). First Samuel 18:1 says that their souls were knit together and that Jonathan loved David as his own soul. When they learned that they would not see each other again, they both wept—David wept the most (1 Sam. 20:41).

As well as some close Christian friends, talk to your parents. Talk to your pastor. Talk to older, godly Christians. Talk to yourself. Dr. Martyn Lloyd-Jones used to ask, "Do you realize that most of your unhappiness is because you are listening to yourself and not talking to yourself?"[1] In the Old Testament, the prophet Jeremiah talked to himself: "'The LORD is my portion,' says my soul, 'Therefore I hope in Him!'" (Lam. 3:24). Instead of despairing during tough times, he would remind himself that God was his.

Above all, talk to God. God knows what we are going through and says He will draw near to us: "The LORD is near to those who have a broken heart, and saves such as have a contrite spirit" (Ps. 34:18). The Psalms are full of people who pour out their souls to God and talk to Him about their troubles. Someone has said that while the Bible speaks *to* us, the Psalms speak *for* us. The Lord Jesus lived a human life and knows what it is to suffer—He is able to help us.

As well as talking to other people, be the sort of young man in whom others can confide. Look out for those who are struggling, whether it be in school or at church. Galatians 6:2

---

1. D. Martyn Lloyd-Jones, *Spiritual Depression: Its Causes and Cures* (New York: HarperCollins, 1998), 20.

tells us to "bear one another's burdens." Be a loyal and trustworthy friend. Develop positive listening skills. Let others talk and tell their story without interrupting them. Ask them to repeat their story, as the second or third time they tell it, they will tend to repeat only the things that trouble them most—then, the real problem will become clearer. As they talk, pray that God would give you wisdom in what to say and that He would remind you of helpful Scripture verses. Point them to God's Word. They may need to be reminded of or introduced to a particular doctrine, encouraged by a promise, or commanded to fulfill a duty. Another practical tip is to walk and talk, as most boys find it easier to talk openly shoulder to shoulder rather than face-to-face.

23

LISTEN

....

As a young man, I thought that I knew everything and that older people were out of touch. Over the last twenty-five years as a teacher, I realize that what was true of me is true of most young men. Mark Twain summed it up well:

> When I was a boy of fourteen, my father was so ignorant I could hardly stand to have the old man around. But when I got to be twenty-one, I was astonished at how much the old man had learned in seven years!

As young men, it is imperative that you *listen* to those older than you, especially your parents. Proverbs 1:8 says, "My son, hear the instruction of your father, and do not forsake the law of your mother." Likewise, Paul writes, "Children, obey your parents in all things, for this is well pleasing to the Lord" (Col. 3:20).

The Lord Jesus Christ obeyed His mother and father. At the age of twelve, during His first trip to Jerusalem for the Passover, Jesus's parents lost Him for three days. At such an important festival time, there would have been several famous Jewish teachers at the feast, and when His frantic parents eventually found Him, Jesus was among these teachers, who were all amazed at His understanding and answers. Having just shown them and others His brilliance, you might think that Jesus would continue preparing for His public ministry by studying under the teachers at the temple in Jerusalem, the center of Jewish religion and politics. He could have accessed its history, law courts, libraries, and leaders. But He didn't. His parents could no longer understand Him, but He returned submissively to Nazareth with them (Luke 2:50–51). Although He was perfect, He dutifully obeyed His imperfect parents.

We must do the same. In our culture, it is almost a given that teenagers rebel. But no one has the right to break the fifth commandment (Ex. 20:12), no matter what our friends or hormones tell us. Independence, thinking for yourself, trying, and failing are all part of growing up. However, stubbornness, rebellion, and disobedience are not. The command to honor one's parents is not only for those who happen to like mom and dad. We don't just listen to them when it suits us or when we agree with what they say. Unless parents command what God forbids (Acts 5:29), we should obey them.

This respect for our parents should also extend to older people and those in positions of authority (1 Peter 5:5). In our day and age, we seldom think, *This person is older and probably has something to teach me*, but rather, *This person is older and out of date*. The younger generations do not know it all. According to Proverbs 20:29, "the glory of young men is their strength, and the splendor of old men is their gray head." Young men may have energy and strength, but older men have knowledge, experience, and wisdom. The apostle Paul writes, "Let the elders who rule well be counted worthy of double honor, especially those who labor in the word and doctrine" (1 Tim. 5:17).

Today we think we know best, and we act as if the two-thousand-year-old church has been waiting for us to arrive on the scene. Lost among all our Tweets, Instagram posts, and blogs is the older generation, who has faithfully stood and plodded on for the last fifty years. We ought to follow the advice given in Proverbs 13:1: "A wise son heeds his father's instruction, but a scoffer does not listen to rebuke."

In my experience, the older generation seems to know God in a way that I don't and to have proved Him in a way that I haven't. Over the last few years, many people in this generation that I have known, loved, and admired have died and gone to glory. I am quite conscious that others may soon join them. It is important that we listen to these older saints while we have them—but not so that they can scold us and reminisce about the good old days. With more distractions, worldliness, and ungodliness in our culture, it is challenging to stand as a young Christian man today. But by listening to our elders, learning how they have proved God, and heeding their advice, we will attain a higher view of God, a greater reverence of Him, a greater desire for Him, and a resolve to truly pursue Him.

So, I encourage you to seek out older, godly Christians in your churches. And by reading books, listen to your spiritual forefathers, whom you will one day meet: the Puritans, the Reformers, George Whitefield, Charles and John Wesley, Charles Spurgeon, Dr. Martyn Lloyd-Jones, and many others.

24

CAST

....

Life is full of worries and stress. If the bravest word a young man can say is "help," then the best thing he can do is *cast*: cast all his worries on the Lord Jesus Christ.

Stop pretending you can do it all yourself. Your circumstances are too much for you, so why not cast all your cares upon Jesus Christ? He is sovereign and controls everything. He holds the heavens and the earth in His hand. Nations rise and fall at His command. Your past, present, and future are all under His control. He created the world, and He will decide when it ends. We often say that God is our Father. But think about it the other way around: Our Father is God!

Children often brag about their fathers. One will say, "My dad can throw a football about a mile!" Another will say, "My dad makes a million trillion dollars a year," to which yet another responds, "That's nothing—mine makes a million trillion dollars a day!" Imagine a dad who could throw a football infinitely far and who owned all the money in every bank in the world. Jesus says, "My Father…is greater than all" (John 10:29). And through faith in Jesus, His Father is also your Father. God is wise, loving, and kind, so He will do what is best for you. He is the King of kings, and although He runs the universe, His eye is upon you.

During Sam Rayburn's tenure as forty-third speaker of the U.S. House of Representatives, the teenage daughter of a reporter he knew died suddenly.[1] The next morning, the reporter heard a knock on his apartment door, opened the door, and found Rayburn standing there. Rayburn said, "I just came by to see what I could do to help." The reporter, stuttering and trying to collect himself, indicated that there was nothing the speaker could do—they were making all the arrangements. Rayburn inquired, "Well, have you all had your coffee this morning?" The reporter confessed that they hadn't had time to do that yet. "Well, I can at least make the coffee this morning," Rayburn said. He went in and made his way to the kitchen in search of coffee. While Rayburn was busy making the coffee, the reporter remembered that Rayburn usually had a standing weekly appointment on this particular morning. So, he inquired, "Mr. Speaker, I thought you were supposed to be having breakfast at the White House this morning." "Well, I was," admitted Rayburn, "but I called the President and told him I had a friend who was in trouble and I couldn't come."

God has a world to run. He has a moon, a sun, stars, and planets to uphold and nations to oversee, but His priority is all those who trust Him and cast their cares upon Him—especially those who are in need. He will look after them. As Peter writes, "Humble yourselves under the mighty hand of God, that He may exalt you in due time, casting all your care upon Him, for He cares for you" (1 Peter 5:6–7).

---

1. Paul F. Boller, *Congressional Anecdotes* (New York: Oxford University Press, 1991), 261.

25

BELONG

As young Christian men, you must *belong* to a local church. The church is not a building but the true people of God, in heaven and on earth. Christ loves the church and gave Himself for her, whom He calls His bride (Eph. 5:25–33). The church was His idea (Matt. 16:18). On the cross, the Lord wasn't saving random men and women to enjoy individual relationships with Himself—He was saving a people.

The church appears in the form of local congregations, each one a microcosm of the universal church. The New Testament assumes that all Christians will share in the life of the local church, worshiping with it (Heb. 10:25), accepting its nurture and discipline (Matt. 18:15–20; Gal. 6:1), and sharing in its work of witnessing to the world.

Christians disobey God when they don't join a local church, and they miss out by not meeting with other Christians. The local church is our family—we ought to use our gifts to help one another. The question is, as there seem to be so many different types of churches, what sort of church should we join?

We should join a church that believes and teaches the Bible as the Word of God from cover to cover; believes that only through faith in Christ alone can a person be right with God; proclaims the gospel; believes that preaching is the primary means ordained by God through which to communicate the gospel; is reverent in worship; sees the necessity of prayer; loves the lost; loves each other; regularly administers the Lord's Supper (Acts 20:7–11); and sings (Eph. 5:19).

It is important to join a healthy, sound church—to be doctrinally correct and to stand against error. For this the Ephesian church was commended (Rev. 2:2–4). We ought to measure everything that is taught and that occurs in our churches against the Word of God, the Bible. We are to be discerning and to be careful that heresy (false teaching) doesn't enter our churches. The church at Thyatira was rebuked because it lacked such discernment (Rev. 2:20–29). Every book you read, every sermon you listen to, every service you attend, every event that takes place in, or is organized by, your church—you must measure all of these against the Word of God. It is vitally important to be sound and discerning.

However, that alone is not enough. There are many sound, theologically correct churches today that have no real love for Jesus Christ. It is as if they've dried up and gone cold. The love they once had has been lost. Above all else, the Lord Jesus wants His church to love Him—indeed, we ought to do everything else *because* we love Him (Rev. 2:4–5). Here are some questions you should ask to discern whether your church loves Christ: Do we delight in reading the Bible? Do we spend time in prayer? Do we love other Christians? Are we troubled that so many of our friends, family members, classmates, and coworkers are on their way to eternal darkness? Do we keep God's commandments because we want to please Him?

Belonging to a church means that you are not a consumer—you don't attend worship on Sunday to get what you can out of it. You must use your gifts to support the church's work. The church is a body, and like a body, each part has a vital role to play—no role is more important than another. It is imperative that we fulfill our roles for the good of the whole church (1 Corinthians 12; Eph. 4:11–15). Peter writes, "As each one has received a gift, minister it to one another, as good stewards of the manifold grace of God" (1 Peter 4:10).

26

FORGET

Many Christians are miserable because they have committed a sin that they do not think can be forgiven—maybe once, maybe more than once, maybe many, many times. Their past, which may or may not have involved other people, haunts them and paralyzes them.

Perhaps this describes you. You've sinned against your Savior many times. You still love Him, but you can't believe that He still loves you. Or if He does, He does so grudgingly, and you can never be close to Him. You think you cannot participate in church life because of your failings. You think you are too bad. You've committed the same sin too many times. You've settled in sin. You're dishonest, lustful, foulmouthed, angry, short-tempered, drunk, selfish, mean, and unkind. Perhaps you've lived a double life—you're a hypocrite, saying one thing but doing another. You've been raised in a Christian home and have enjoyed lots and lots of privileges. You've heard hundreds of sermons and have been to a Christian camp every summer, but you've sinned despite all of this.

God does not want you to feel this way and remain in this sorry state. However, you must tell Him everything—search your heart and hide nothing Him. It will be painful, but it is the only way to be fully restored and to enjoy intimate communion with the Savior. Confess and repent of any known sin (1 John 1:8–9). You can always be honest with God. You don't have to put on an act or show Him your social media profile. He knows you better than you know yourself. There is nothing you can tell Him that He doesn't already know.

But then you must believe that He has forgiven you, *forget* the past, and get on with living the Christian life. The apostle Paul writes, "But one thing I do, forgetting those things which are behind and reaching forward to those things which are ahead, I press toward the goal for the prize of the upward call of God in Christ Jesus" (Phil. 3:13–14).

Forgetting sin is not passive. You have to actively obliterate any thoughts of the past. You forget! You don't keep trying to reverse the irreversible consequence of your sins—even the "big one"—the tragic mistakes that have disfigured your life. You confess them all to God and trust that He will forgive and cover your sins as He has promised (Pss. 32:1–2; 85:2; Rom. 4:7–8; 1 John 1:9). It is not even helpful to keep praying about them. According to Lloyd-Jones, "There are particular problems in the Christian life that if you do nothing but pray about them you will never solve them. You must stop praying at times because your prayer may just be reminding you of the problem and keeping your mind fixed upon it."[1]

I am pretty sure that the following story is not true, but the principle definitely is (Ps. 25:7; Heb. 8:12). Apparently,

---

1. D. Martyn Lloyd-Jones, *Spiritual Depression: Its Causes and Cure* (Grand Rapids: Eerdmans, 1965), 69.

there was a woman in the Philippines who claimed to talk to God. Her priest, to test her, told her to ask God about the sins of his youth. The following week, he asked her what God had said. She replied, "He doesn't remember!"

God has forgotten the sins that you have asked Him to forgive. You, too, should *forget*.

27

PERSEVERE

Making a decision for Jesus Christ is not enough. Many people have had a moment, even a period, where they have wanted to become a Christian. Maybe they were at a Christian camp or a moving church service. But the parable of the sower (Matt. 13:1–9) teaches that there are people who hear the gospel, immediately receive it with joy, and live the Christian life for a while—but when tribulation or persecution arises on account of the gospel, they fall away immediately. Others give up quickly because of the cares of the world and the deceitfulness of riches.

You can start out well, but the test of whether you are saved is that you *persevere*. No one receives the gospel with the intention of falling away. In 1 Corinthians 9:24, the apostle Paul writes, "Do you not know that those who run in a race all run, but one receives the prize? Run in such a way that you may obtain it." Likewise, Hebrews 3:6–19 teaches that the proof of your salvation is your perseverance. The only guarantee that you are a Christian is that you endure to the very end. The Christian life is fraught with trials, temptations, and difficulties. The world will constantly pull you back, but only those who persevere will be saved.

Do not assume that if you go to church now and take some interest in spiritual things, then you always will. The mistake that many make, which they will eternally regret, is to treat God and His salvation casually and to think that they can return to it at a more convenient time in the future. Growing up, I attended the Evangelical Movement of Wales conference in Aberystwyth. I wasn't a Christian, and I would go with other boys to a licensed café every night after most people had gone to bed. We would drink beer and get into all sorts of trouble. Most of us were elders' and ministers' sons. Every one of us at the time would have believed the things we heard preached, but we wanted to have our fun and intended to take these things more seriously later on in our lives. Thirty years later, out of about twenty of us, only two or three have any interest in Jesus Christ.

Only those who are living the Christian life now and who endure until the end will be saved. Like the apostle Paul, make sure you can say on your deathbed, "I have fought the good fight, I have finished the race, I have kept the faith" (2 Tim. 4:7).

Daley Thompson was a gold medalist in the 1984 Los Angeles Olympics. His event was the decathlon which comprises ten track-and-field events. The last event is the 1,500-meter run. After Thompson won the gold medal, an interviewer asked him how he felt before this final event. He replied, "I thought about the gold medal and told myself, 'Whatever it takes!'" When temptation comes, when sin and the world seem so attractive, when persecution arises, when the going gets so tough that you're about to give up—think about the prize and tell yourself, "Whatever it takes."

28

LEAD

....

Young men must be prepared to *lead*. If and when you get married, you will be required to lead your wife and family (Eph. 5:22–23). You may be called upon to lead in your church or in your workplace. You will need to be brave, selfless, and decisive.

Today, the idea of wives "submitting" (Eph. 5:22) to their husbands is seen as archaic, offensive, and misogynistic. Moreover, in the world of work, men have selfishly abused their power. But the biblical pattern of leadership is not meant to be offensive or demeaning, nor does it mean that men can lord it over people in an aggressive, chauvinistic, pugnacious way.

Husbands are required to love their wives as Christ loved the church (Eph. 5:25). They are meant to lead in such a way that wives will find it easy to submit. They are to be unselfish, kind, caring, and protective.

This is in stark contrast with the thinking of Christ's day. At that time, rabbis refused to teach women and generally treated them as inferiors. They thought it was better to burn the law than to teach it to a woman. Women were not trusted to give testimony in a court of law. Aristotle and Socrates also held women in low esteem. But Jesus freely admitted them into His fellowship and assigned them a place of high honor. While the Bible recognizes that men and women are different and that they have distinct roles to play within the church, nothing has done more for the dignity of women than the Christian faith. But we must not swap the roles of men and women—we must not try to make women significant by giving them men's duties. The roles of men and women are different but equally important.

Growing up, I had three heroes: my dad, my uncle, and my grandfather. They were hardworking, selfless, and kind. They told good stories, laughed a lot, enjoyed sports, and liked people for who they were, not for what they did. My dad always made sure that my mom, my sisters, and I were okay before he looked after himself. He protected and provided for us. Having "stuff" wasn't important to him, but family, friends, and a house full of laughter were. He did the right thing, not the easiest thing, and had a sense of duty. These were qualities I thought were "manly," and when I grew older, I wanted to be just like these men. They put God first and realized that they were answerable to Him. In our house, there was a plaque that read, "Christ is the head of this house, the unseen guest at every mealtime, the silent listener to every conversation."

Another example of true, manly leadership is the All Blacks rugby team—arguably the greatest sports team in the world. They have a saying about "sweeping the sheds." It means that however good a player you are, and however big a superstar you become, you are never too important to do the small things, such as cleaning the changing rooms after a muddy match.

But the ultimate example of manly leadership is recorded in John 13:1–15, on the night Jesus was betrayed. In the upper room, thirteen men (Jesus and His twelve disciples) would have been gathered around a short table, reclining on cushions on the floor. They had just walked to Jerusalem from Bethany, and their feet would have been dirty, smelly, and sore. It was a servant's job to wash people's feet. This was the most menial of all his tasks. Just imagine washing off the sweat and grime from people's feet after they have walked in sandals along those dirty, dusty roads. Indeed, anything to do with feet was seen as the lowest of the low. To emphasize his inferiority to Jesus, John the Baptist said that he was not even worthy to carry His sandals (Matt. 3:11).

In the upper room would have stood the pitcher, together with the washbasin and the linen cloth, but there was no servant to carry out this task. The disciples had just been arguing about who was the greatest (Luke 22:24), and every one of them would have viewed this job as totally beneath him. But no one expected what happened next, which left an indelible impression on John's mind. As he writes his gospel years later, he remembers every detail.

The Lord Jesus Christ, the eternal Son of God and the Creator of the universe, put on a slave's apron, poured water into a basin, and washed the disciples' feet one by one. Even when He got to Judas—the man who would betray Him to

His enemies in a few hours—He took his dirty feet, washed them, and wiped them with the towel tied around His waist.

By washing His disciples' feet, Christ showed these men what true greatness and servant-hearted leadership looks like. It isn't about sitting in the places of honor and lording it over people—it's about esteeming others more highly than yourself and putting their needs before your own. Christ doesn't view greatness in terms of power, wealth, or status. He views greatness in terms of humility and selflessness.

The evidence that someone is a real Christian is found in how they see themselves and how they treat others. J. K. Rowling wrote, "If you want to know what a man's like, take a good look at how he treats his inferiors."[1]

---

1. J. K. Rowling, *Harry Potter and the Goblet of Fire* (New York: Arthur A. Levine, 2000), 525.

29

GO

In Matthew 28:19, Jesus commissions His disciples to make disciples of all nations—men, women, boys, and girls who will follow the Lord Jesus Christ. To do that, the disciples needed to *go* into the world.

Today, as young Christian men, you must do the same in your schools, universities, workplaces, and neighborhoods. Share the gospel with your friends and family. Invite people to church. Witness by how you live and what you say. Go to wherever people are and talk to them about our Savior—winsomely, urgently, and clearly. You must love people. If you don't have a burden for the lost, then you need to ask God to give you one.

We ought to care as much about evangelism as God does. When Christ saw the multitudes, He had compassion on them (Matt. 9:36)—we need to love others in the same way. We need to go out and declare to unbelievers that there is a God, a judgment, a heaven, and a hell. We need to tell them that they are sinners, but that Jesus Christ died to save sinners. We need to urge them, implore them, plead with them to repent of their sin and trust Him.

This is not easy. I imagine that most of you, if not all of you, are embarrassed to evangelize. You worry what people will say and think, you don't want to be mocked or ostracized, and you think that they just won't believe. In his letter to the Romans, Paul writes, "For I am not ashamed of the gospel of Christ, for it is the power of God to salvation for everyone who believes, for the Jew first and also for the Greek" (Rom. 1:16). Paul was clearly aware of the general contempt in which the gospel is held. A man would not say that he is unashamed of something unless he had been tempted to feel ashamed of it. The Lord Jesus told His disciples not to be ashamed of Him, anticipating that they might be (Matt. 10:32–33; Mark 8:38; Luke 9:26). Paul knew this temptation. In Acts 18:9, God said to Paul, "Do not be afraid."

As Paul writes to these Roman Christians, he is confident in the gospel. He wants them to know that there is no reason to be ashamed of it and that he is ready to preach it everywhere, even in Rome (1:15–16). This confidence had nothing to do with Paul in and of himself. He was no superman. In fact, according to tradition, Paul was an ugly little guy with beetle brows, bowlegs, a bald head, a hooked nose, bad eyesight, and no rhetorical gifts, which seems to confirm what Paul said of himself in 2 Corinthians 10:10 and Galatians 4:13. He even described himself as "less than the least of all the saints" (Eph. 3:8). He felt totally unworthy. But Paul was an apostle (Rom. 1:1, 5), commissioned by God to preach the gospel, and while he had a minute view of himself, he had a magnificent view of the gospel. As he writes to the Romans, he reminds them of its power. They boasted about their power to conquer the world—but the gospel is far superior. It comes from God (Rom. 1:1), the God who made the whole world.

History has proven the power of the gospel. By the close of the apostolic period (the time of the New Testament), there were close to half a million Christians in the world. A bunch of unremarkable people, by the power of the Holy Spirit, had turned the world upside down (Acts 17:6). According to Dr. Martyn Lloyd-Jones,

> The unvarnished gospel possessed by a little group of men and women having apparently no influence or power challenged the great Roman empire so that it began to totter and shake until it eventually fell while this small body of people continued to grow and increase and spread throughout the world.[1]

So, if you are ostracized, mocked, persecuted, or pitied because of your faith, remember the power of the gospel. Don't be ashamed of it—rely on it.

I taught with a man whom I absolutely loved. He had one of the best laughs I have ever heard. I remember sitting in the staff room with him and just laughing and laughing and laughing. He retired and, within a few months, became terminally ill. I never spoke to him about my Savior. I never told him clearly that Jesus died on the cross and rose again that all our sins may be forgiven. Even when I saw him just before he died, I didn't urge him to repent and believe the gospel. I was too embarrassed; I didn't want to offend him. I can't be sure

---

1. Iain H. Murray, *D. Martyn Lloyd-Jones, vol. 1, The First Forty Years, 1899–1939* (Edinburgh: Banner of Truth, 1982), 139.

where he is now, but if he has gone to a lost eternity, those laughs aren't doing him any good. If he saw me, he would no doubt ask, "Why didn't you tell me?"

Importantly, we need to proclaim the gospel in all the nations (Matt. 28:19). "For God so loved the *world*" (John 3:16). Maybe some of you reading this book will be called to *go* to foreign lands and serve as missionaries. But today, in countries like Britain, the nations have come to us. We need to go to these people—many of them have never heard the gospel.

A missionary spoke at the Heath Evangelical Church in Cardiff a few years ago. He told us about his parents, who were among the first missionaries to go to Indonesia. As these Indonesians were told about the cross and the resurrection, many hundreds of them were saved. One of the tribal chiefs asked the missionaries: How long ago did Jesus die? Last week? Last month? Last year? When the missionaries said that He died two thousand years ago, the people couldn't believe it and asked them why it had taken them so long to bring the gospel to Indonesia!

30

ASK

None of us can live the Christian life by our own strength. We must ask God to help us and give us the power of the Holy Spirit. The book of Hebrews was written to Christians who were about to abandon the faith. The writer tells them in Hebrews 4:14 to "hold fast"—not to give in and not to give up. He isn't simply trying to motivate them. He gives them a reason: they have a great High Priest. He writes,

> Seeing then that we have a great High Priest who has passed through the heavens, Jesus the Son of God, let us hold fast our confession. For we do not have a High Priest who cannot sympathize with our weaknesses, but was in all points tempted as we are, yet without sin. Let us therefore come boldly to the throne of grace, that we may obtain mercy and find grace to help in time of need. (Heb. 4:14–16)

In the old covenant, the high priest represented the people before God. However, because of Christ's work on the cross, there is no need for priests anymore. Jesus Christ is our great High Priest, and we can approach God directly through Him. In order to represent the people before God, the high priest needed to fully understand and sympathize with them. Because Jesus lived in this world for thirty-three years and suffered the way He did, He can fully sympathize with every one of us—He is our sympathetic High Priest.

The Bible says that Jesus learned obedience (Heb. 5:8). He was perfect, so this cannot mean that He learned how to be good. It means that He learned what it was like to be human. He learned what it was like to be me and you. The Lord Jesus is now in heaven, sitting at the Father's right hand. When I pray to Him for help, He must be as close as possible to the Father. But at the same time, He must remember what it was like to be me. His time on earth, and on the cross, means that He does. When I feel like giving up, when the temptations and trials around me seem overwhelming, I must go to Him for help, knowing that He is willing and able to intercede for me.

I grew up in a place called Ebbw Vale. Our local member of parliament was Michael Foot. He was the leader of the Labour Party and would sit across the dispatch box in the House of Commons from the prime minister, Mrs. Thatcher. He was right at the center of it all, but he never forgot what it was like on the backstreets of Ebbw Vale and Brynmawr and Tredegar. He was in Westminster, but those South Wales valley towns and villages were on his mind.

Jesus Christ is in heaven, but as I pray to Him from my bedroom, school, university, church—from anywhere—He represents my cause, remembering exactly what it is like to be me. We must therefore go boldly to the throne of God and *ask* for grace in times of need (Heb. 4:16).

APPENDIX

*A four-year reading plan for young
Christian men (see chapter 11)*

Year 1

Book 1 – Peter Jeffrey, *Walk Worthy: Guidelines for the Christian Faith*

Book 2 – Peter Jeffrey, *All Things New: A Help for Those Beginning the Christian Life*

Book 3 – Peter Jeffrey, *Christian Handbook: A Straightforward Guide to the Bible, Church History and Christian Doctrine*

Book 4 – J. C. Ryle, *Expository Thoughts on Matthew*

Book 5 – J. I. Packer, *Concise Theology: A Guide to Historic Christian Beliefs*

Book 6 – John Bunyan, *The Pilgrim's Progress*

Book 7 – Dale Ralph Davis, *Joshua: No Falling Words*

Book 8 – Arnold A. Dallimore, *Spurgeon: A Biography*

Book 9 – Stuart Olyott, *Daniel: Dare to Stand Alone*

Book 10 – J. Gresham Machen, *The New Testament: An Introduction to Its Literature and History*

Year 2

Book 1 – Kris A. Lundgaard, *The Enemy Within: Straight Talk About the Power and Defeat of Sin*

Book 2 – Mary Drewery, *Richard Wurmbrand: The Man Who Came Back*

Book 3 – D. Martyn Lloyd-Jones, *Studies in the Sermon on the Mount*

Book 4 – J. C. Ryle, *Expository Thoughts on Mark*

Book 5 – J. I. Packer, *"Fundamentalism" and the Word of God*

Book 6 – Roland H. Bainton, *Here I Stand: A Life of Martin Luther*

Book 7 – J. C. Ryle, *Holiness*

Book 8 – J. C. Ryle, *Expository Thoughts on John*

Year 3

Book 1 – John Calvin, *Truth for All Time*

Book 2 – Thomas Watson, *A Body of Divinity*

Book 3 – D. Martyn Lloyd-Jones, *Spiritual Depression: Its Causes and Cure*

Book 4 – Dale Ralph Davis, *Judges: Such a Great Salvation*

Book 5 – J. C. Ryle, *Christian Leaders of the Eighteenth Century*

Book 6 – J. I. Packer, *Knowing God*

Book 7 – Michael Reeves, *Enjoy Your Prayer Life*

Book 8 – John Murray, *Redemption Accomplished and Applied*

Book 9 – Stuart Olyott, *Romans: The Gospel As It Really Is*

Book 10 – Edward Donnelly, *Heaven and Hell*

Year 4

Book 1 – Dale Ralph Davis, *1 Samuel: Looking on the Heart*
Book 2 – Dale Ralph Davis, *2 Samuel: Out of Every Adversity*
Book 3 – A. W. Tozer, *The Pursuit of God*
Book 4 – David Wilkerson, John Sherrill, and Elizabeth Sherrill, *The Cross and the Switchblade: The True Story of One Man's Fearless Faith*
Book 5 – Dale Ralph Davis, *1 Kings: The Wisdom and the Folly*
Book 6 – Dale Ralph Davis, *2 Kings: The Power and the Fury*
Book 7 – Peter Barnes, *John Calvin: Man of God's Word*
Book 8 – Dane C. Ortlund, *Gentle and Lowly: The Heart of Christ for Sinners and Sufferers*
Book 9 – Brian H. Edwards, *Revival: A People Saturated with God*
Book 10 – Kevin DeYoung, *The Good News We Almost Forgot: Rediscovering the Gospel in a 16th Century Catechism*

BIBLIOGRAPHY

Blanchard, John. *Major Points from the Minor Prophets*. Darlington, UK: Evangelical Press, 2012.

Boller, Paul F. *Congressional Anecdotes*. New York: Oxford University Press, 1991.

Calvin, John. *Commentary on a Harmony of the Evangelists, Matthew, Mark, and Luke*. Edinburgh: Calvin Translation Society, 1845.

———. *Institutes of the Christian Religion*. Translated by Robert White. Edinburgh: Banner of Truth, 2014.

Carson, D. A., ed. *From Sabbath to Lord's Day: A Biblical, Historical and Theological Investigation*. Eugene, Ore.: Wipf and Stock, 1999.

Christofides, Andrew. *The Life Sentence*. Milton Keynes, UK: Paternoster Press, 2002.

Kuyper, Abraham. "Sphere Sovereignty." In *Abraham Kuyper: A Centennial Reader*. Edited by James D. Bratt. Grand Rapids: Eerdmans, 1998.

Lewis, C. S. *Mere Christianity*. New York: HarperCollins, 2009.

Lloyd-Jones, D. Martyn. *Spiritual Depression: Its Causes and Cure*. Grand Rapids: Eerdmans, 1965.

Lloyd-Jones, D. Martyn. *Spiritual Depression: Its Causes and Cures*. New York: HarperCollins, 1998.

Maier, Paul L., trans. *Josephus: The Essential Writings*. Grand Rapids: Kregel, 1988.

Montgomery, James. "Prayer Is the Soul's Sincere Desire." 1818.

Murray, Iain H. *D. Martyn Lloyd-Jones*. Vol. 1, *The First Forty Years, 1899–1939*. Edinburgh: Banner of Truth, 1982.

Olyott, Stuart. *Something Must Be Known and Felt: A Missing Note in Today's Christianity*. Bangor, UK: Bryntirion Press, 2014.

Packer, J. I. *Concise Theology: A Guide to Historic Christian Beliefs*. London: Inter-Varsity Press, 1994.

Palmer, H. R. "Yield Not to Temptation." 1868.

Roberts, Vaughan. *Battles Christians Face: Tackling Big Issues with Confidence*. Second edition. Milton Keynes, UK: Authentic Media, 2013.

Rowling, J. K. *Harry Potter and the Goblet of Fire*. New York: Arthur A. Levine, 2000.

Stibbs, Alan M., ed. *Search the Scriptures: A Three-Year Daily Devotional Guide to the Whole Bible*. Downers Grove, Ill.: InterVarsity Press, 2004.

Stone, Jay. "Carrey's Been Busted." *Ottawa Citizen*. December 16, 2005.

Thomas, Dylan. "Do Not Go Gentle into That Good Night," https://www.poetryfoundation.org/poems/46569/do-not-go-gentle-into-that-good-night.

Thomas, I. D. E., comp. *The Golden Treasury of Puritan Quotations*. Edinburgh: Banner of Truth, 2000.

Toplady, Augustus. "Rock of Ages." 1776.

Tozer, A. W. *The Pursuit of God*. London: Marshall, Morgan & Scott, 1961.

Wilkinson, Jonny. "Jonny Wilkinson: Winning Has Its Drawbacks." *The Times*. November 21, 2009. https://www.thetimes.co.uk/article/jonny-wilkinson-winning-has-its-drawbacks-g2jwn22p72c.